voice lessons

voice

lessons

On
Becoming
a
(Woman)
Writer

nancy mairs

BEACON PRESS · BOSTON

Beacon Press
25 Beacon Street
Boston, Massachusetts 02108-2892

Beacon Press books
are published under the auspices of
the Unitarian Universalist Association of Congregations.

Some of the material in these essays has appeared in the following:
*The American Voice, Anima, The Cream City Review, Frontiers,
New York Times Book Review, The Ohio Review, Poets & Writers,*
and one of my earlier books, *Remembering the Bone House: An
Erotics of Place and Space.* The excerpt from "Spring" from *House
of Light* by Mary Oliver, copyright © 1990 by Mary Oliver, is
reprinted by permission of Beacon Press.

99 98 97 96 95 94   8 7 6 5 4 3 2

Text design by Christine Raquepaw

Library of Congress Cataloging-in-Publication Data

Mairs, Nancy, 1943–
    Voice lessons : on becoming a (woman) writer / Nancy Mairs.
      p.   cm.
    Includes bibliographical references (p.   ).
    ISBN 0–8070–6006–2
    1. Mairs, Nancy, 1943–.   2. Women authors, American—20th
century—Biography.   3. Authorship—Sex differences.   4. Women
and literature.   I. Title.
PS3563.A386Z478   1994
818'.5409—dc20
    [B]   93–31513

For Sally Smith Caroline,

sister by birth,

and Susan Hardy Aiken,

sister in spirit,

who have listened long and closely

Contents

CONTENTS

viii

Acknowledgments

*a*s I was putting the finishing touches on this book, a reviewer of my last one, *Ordinary Time*, wrote: "I'd like to hear Mairs take more responsibility for her literary curiosity and its consequences." The end of a writing project fills me with melancholy misgivings, and I'm grateful to her for reassuring me, however unwittingly, that at least one person will think I've spent these last months doing as I ought.

From this reader, unknown to me, my gratitude leaps back more than thirty years, to those who aroused my literary curiosity in the first place while accepting my literary ambitions with perfect gravity. Hazel Bullis, who despite her execrable taste in literature (she made us ninth-graders read

"Sohrab and Rustum," for heaven's sake) taught me every possible permutation of the English sentence. Helena Corbett in high school, who failed the first paragraph I wrote for her because, though exquisitely composed, it bore no relation to the assignment. My college English professors: Charles Aughtry (who was spied by my roommate tearing through the corridors brandishing the "fuck" I used in my paper on "A Streetcar Named Desire"), Edwin Briggs (who introduced me to Virginia Woolf), Katherine Burr (for whom I wrote my own "Essay on Man," so help me God), Curtis Dahl ("many trees but few leaves" he wrote beside the 77 he gave me on my Victorian literature final), Louise Barr MacKenzie (who scoffed at my "little lyric cries"), Robert Sharp (who made me love Adam and Eve and their lost garden), and Robert Taylor (who showed up to celebrate when I won the Western States Book Award twenty years later). Severe mentors all, they made reading and writing strenuous enough to seem worth doing.

Though my dear editor, Andrew Hrycyna, wasn't even alive during most of these goings on, he captures their spirit perfectly in his always fruitful questions and chastisements. For his clear and steady vision of this book by/about/for the lover of the word, my deepest thanks.

Nancy Mairs
Tucson, Spring 1993

Prelude: Loving the Other

Other-Love is writing's first name.

—Hélène Cixous, "Sorties"

"*a*nd if you're very, very lucky, like me," I wrote to my daughter several years ago as she made her leisurely way from a Peace Corps stint in Zaïre to Tucson to begin whatever-came-next, "you'll wind up with a perfect life!" I really did, and do, believe that my life is perfect, although I recognize that certain details of it—like my own advancing debilitation by multiple sclerosis and my husband's metastatic melanoma—might seem from the outside to forbid it such status and even to mark me as (1) a Pollyanna, to use a quaint term, (2) in denial, as pop-psych-speak would have it, or (3), to be blunt, out of my wits.

"The outside," however, never provides a good vantage

point for life study. The truth is that (1) I would look on the bright side of anything only if it were illuminated from every direction simultaneously, and I'm still waiting for such a curiosity to occur; (2) I know perfectly well that I've got MS and George has cancer, though I'd be glad to take a break from these facts if I could just figure out how all those "co-dependents" get denial to work; and (3) since they're all I've got to live by, I'm into my wits right up to my eyebrows. The truth is also that although "perfect" may mean "flawless," it may mean "consummate" or "whole" as well, and it is in this sense that I cherish my life as I could not, perhaps, without its flaws. That is, these force me to live daily at the potential end of the world as I know it, and so, on any given day, my life must be as fully made as I can make it: perfect.

This view implies considerably more satisfaction than I could have admitted to during my first forty years, but whether I would adopt it now if I hadn't become a writer I don't know. I suspect not. Certainly there was never another end I longed for more persistently, or with a greater sense of futility, from at least the time I was thirteen and listed "writer" as my "future profession" in my junior high school literary magazine. As my life unfolded, I believed that I could be, and then became, a college girl, a wife, a mother, a technical editor, a graduate student, a teacher. I even became some things I could never have believed—for six months when I was in my early twenties, I was an inmate in a state mental hospital—and managed to come to terms with them. But a writer seemed another and altogether elusive order of being: I didn't know how to become her. Is it any wonder then that when I come out to my studio each day and flip on my computer—for which I traded, some years ago, my beloved fountain pens and yellow legal-size pads—I feel as though I've died and gone to heaven? Perhaps in this light you will forgive my use of "perfect" to describe my life.

An anonymous reader of an early version of this book, about whom I know only that "she" is "an academic," concluded: "It is obvious from her criticism that she wasn't meant to be an academic, from her encounter with French feminist theory, that she wasn't cut out for a career as a critic. What is obvious is that she is a real writer." I could have wept, if frustration any longer had the power to elicit the tears reserved now for anguish unspeakably deeper. In a single sentence she reimposed the very dichotomies I had constructed the book in order to call into question, putting electrified fences around the categories "academy," "criticism," and "writing" to keep the various critters from intermingling, maybe interbreeding to create some nameless monster very like the one I aspire to be.

And what queer syntax. "Meant" by whom? "Cut out" by whom? Is there a God in the Academy creating academics in His own image and dispensing careers according to some holy plan? If I'm the product of intention, I'd like to know who intended me. And how is a "real" writer distinguished from other sorts (what sorts?) of writers? These are not idle questions. And they do not have merely private significance. The capacity—the drive—to segregate and hierarchize intellectual pursuits, to speak of them in the passive voice as though they were ordained by some anonymous agency, and to envision "real" as a discrete state distinguishable (by the rigorous critical mind) from some other way of being infects otherwise fluid and flexible intelligences with a kind of cerebral tetanus that inhibits *jouissance* before the first lovely ripple of pleasure has fairly begun.

I am not a "real writer." I am a writer. Without modification.

This is a book about becoming a writer. Although it is autobiographical, as my earlier books were, in tracing specifically the formation of a "damned scribbling woman" it is more linear and more literary than they. I've continued to use the essay form, which I like for its power to both focus and disrupt, and the individual essays overlap chronologically to some extent rather than forming discrete links in a narrative chain. (Nevertheless, the earlier essays here do lay out both personal experiences and theoretical premises upon which the later essays rest, and so readers may wish to begin at the beginning.)

What has interested me particularly is the crucial role that learning to decipher texts—both my own experiences and the works of other writers—has played in my writerly evolution. "Lives do not serve as models," Carolyn Heilbrun points out, "only stories do that. And it is a hard thing to make up stories to live by. We can only retell and live by the stories we have read or heard. We live our lives through texts."[1] Texts may be other than printed matter, of course, and nowadays technology produces new media faster than most of us can learn to use them (honestly now, if you're over forty, can you program your VCR, and if so, will you come program mine?), but I am just old enough to have established my primary textual relationship with books. I have been learning to read since I was four or five, but not until more than thirty years later did I discover the texts—I think *The Madwoman in the Attic* was one of the first—

which offered a level of insight enabling me to structure my hitherto chaotic life, captured in diaries and journals as well as memory, into a story that made sense to me and later to others for whom that life also became text. In retrospect, I understand that through this process I made a woman of myself.

Since I have, I confess, succumbed more than once to the ambiguous pleasures of French psychoanalytic and literary theory, be(com)ing a woman has turned out to be a vastly more exciting and unnerving venture than Mother led me to believe. In that venture, she said, there would be the wedding and the loss of my maidenhead (in that order) and the children. What else? Nothing that I can remember. Her own nest wasn't empty yet, so she didn't speak of that, or of debility or despair, though I glimpsed these through grand-mothers and elderly aunts. Womanly existence might seem of questionable import, but it was never itself called into question.

She said little of my becoming a writer and certainly nothing of the tangled relationship to words that such a development would entail. She didn't hint that language, which seemed to be a tool—ordinary to the point of transparency—for representing my daily needs and de-mands and desires, could function as a giant india rubber for effacing the very subject of those needs and demands and desires. "Phallogocentrism," theorists have called this restriction on utterance: the erection of the Word to plug up the hole that holds "the feminine." (Like the seal on a sewer? But if the gasses build up enough, isn't the whole thing gonna *blow*?) The language a woman has planned to use to express her experience turns out, in this scheme, to depend for its very existence and efficacy on her repression.

A discovery of such magnitude—that one has been systematically excluded from life, never mind literature—is enough to knock anyone on her ass. Which was my posture over the last decade or so (and remains so, not just because I live in a wheelchair but because it puts me at the right height in front of my computer). Of course, French is a lubricious language, permitting slippages between "woman" and "female" and "feminine," and so the matter as framed by French theorists is not quite so bad as it might seem. (Or rather, it *is* just as bad as it seems, but for a slightly different population.) As Alice Jardine points out, "Theorists in France continue to emphasize the effects of the human subject's inscription in culture through language—the recognition, for example, that the signifier 'woman' does not necessarily *mean* the biological female in history. 'Woman,' 'the feminine,' and so on have come to signify those *processes* that disrupt symbolic structures in the West."[2] We're all "women" here to some extent.

All the same, I'm American enough to believe that some of us are more so than others: that although "woman" may not *necessarily* mean the biological female, it does to most of us most of the time, and that those of us who happen to be both women and biological females are apt to have distinctive experiences and responses arising from that conjunction. When I think of myself as a writer (and nowadays that's precisely how I do think of myself), I mean as a biologically female feminine woman writer. I think of myself in other specificities as well, reflecting my age, social class, education, physical condition, and so on. I feel suspicious of the generalized Author, which strikes me as the term of choice of a masculine man (but not necessarily biologically male) writer.

That specific "I" is, of course, a construction. I continually make her up as I go along out of whatever materials come to hand. Because I am a writer, these materials tend to be literary (and even when they're not, I tend to "read" them as though they were); for the past ten years or so, they have been predominantly works written by women. It's not that I resist or refuse works by men, but because my education focused on them, I've had a lot of catching up to do. Since I can't keep up with the works by women being published, my bias is more pragmatic than ideological. The essays I've included in this volume illustrate the process whereby I've constructed myself as a writer in relation to some of the (m)others whose writing has aroused me and nurtured and chastised me, each one drawing me on, teaching me to love her, to love myself in her, to love myself, to love: To write.

My purpose in this book, then, is to reflect the ways in which certain voices (of both men and women) trained me and continue to modulate and refine my own. Not surprisingly, the most instructive of these is Virginia Woolf. In my debt to her, as in many other circumstances, I am hardly original, nor do I intend to be. On the contrary, I am concerned with the ways in which my experiences resonate with, rather than depart from, those of my readers. Like Heilbrun, I believe that women, especially, must

> see themselves collectively, not individually, not caught in some individual erotic and familial plot and, inevitably, found wanting. Individual stories from biographies and autobiographies have always been conceived of as individual, eccentric lives. I suspect that female narratives will be found where women exchange stories, where they read and talk collectively of ambitions, and possibilities, and accomplishments.[3]

And of shared passions. If you and I have Virginia Woolf—or Doris Lessing or Alice Walker or Hélène Cixous—in common, so much the better. I only wish I'd had the space to revel in more of the passions I hope we share, especially for Jane Austen and Joan Didion and British detective fiction.

When I published my first book on essays, *Plaintext*, my editor persuaded me to leave out one essay on the grounds that its scholarly tone (though often parodic), together with all the quotations and accompanying notes, would scare off the general reader. He may have been right. But I've always been sorry that we left the essay out because it did a couple of things that the other essays didn't do. It gave credit, for one thing, to a large number of works, especially in feminist theory, which inform all my thinking deeply. More important, by quoting from these works liberally, the essay revealed and paid homage to their charms. Jane Tompkins elucidates this facet of the use of quotations—very different from conventional scholarly usage—in her essay "Me and My Shadow":

> I find that having released myself from the duty to say things I'm not interested in, in a language I resist, I feel free to entertain other people's voices. Quoting them becomes a pleasure of appreciation rather than the obligatory giving of credit, because when I write in a voice that is not struggling to be heard through the screen of forced language, I no longer feel that it is not I who am speaking, and so, there is more room for what others have said.[4]

In this collaborative spirit, I have quoted liberally from works that stimulate me, *with* notes.

Recently, another introverted writer and I were getting through a cocktail party by trying to figure out how we'd come to be the way we are. Neither of us could remember *not* writing, in the sense that from our earlier memories we had watched and narrated to ourselves the stories of ourselves, translating every experience even as it happened into language, or perhaps having no experience at all unless it was translated into language: "and then Nancy . . ."; "and then Barbara. . . ." I'd always assumed that all children consciously make up their lives this way as they go along, but apparently, she'd found recently, they do not. And even if they did, they don't all turn into writers.

What taught *us* to inscribe our imaginings as soon as we had implements and a serviceable code? It came down to the predictable answer: we'd read. Not just for information or for entertainment but for companionship in the narrative adventure. We told ourselves stories and those writers told themselves stories and gradually we started telling their stories and they started telling our stories and there we all were, caught forever in a tangle of language. The (m)others through whom we think back if we are women were thinking their way forward and outward through us.

Perhaps for this reason, writing about the works of other women strikes me as a filial gesture. Except that the word feels wrong on my tongue—"filial." The meaning's all right: "of or relating to a son or daughter." As is so often the case, the bitter twist lies along the root: *filius*, son, from *felare*, to suck, suckle. The son feeds at the mother's breast (oh, and by analogy, the daughter too). Well, we girls will just have to wriggle our way back in there. Howl our hunger. Clap greedy mouths to nipples. Take what nourishment we can from Virginia, from Doris, from Hélène, from Alice. Suckle our daughters. Pour out our store for friends, for students, for readers. Filiate for ourselves.

I sound more essentialist in these reflections—indeed, throughout this book—than I really feel. True, I remain convinced of the power of sexual difference at the corporeal level. I think, for instance, that whether one bears one's genitals on the inside or the outside—although entailing a shift of only a few inches and some minor structural modifications—profoundly affects one's sense of self-sufficiency or vulnerability. All the same, the difference I confront through writing is earlier, more profound, and more grievous: my body is not your body. Regardless of genital arrangements, we are not the same.

And you are the *other* other of these writings. The "you" of my "I." For the first several years of teaching composition, I would not permit my students to write in the first person. Ever. I had been schooled in the evils of subjectivity. I failed my term report in freshman biology because "I" kept talking about "seeing" toppled trees and fungi instead of noting that trees "had fallen" and fungi "had appeared" on their rotting bark. And in typical teacherly fashion I passed this received wisdom along. The students' writing was predictably ghastly. Gradually, as I read more rhetorical theory and personal essays, I permitted, and then encouraged, the use of the first person. Their writing remained ghastly—but measurably less so, I would argue. Comma splices, mixed metaphors, jumpy transitions, adolescent ideologies: bad writing at every level is easier to bear, and to work with, if the writer is *in* it, not holding herself ten thousand light years away in the name of objectivity. For me, pedagogy and practice are always intertwined, and so "I" was entering and inhabiting my own writing more and more openly during this time as well.

Admitting the second person was far more problematic. Except in the imperative, I had been taught never to use it, and hortatory prose had limited usefulness for me or my students. I disliked direct address in my students' work for what I told myself were stylistic but were really social and emotional reasons. It threw me into confrontation, even contact, with them, and I have never cared for either interlocked gaze or touch. If I permitted my students the "you" as well as the "I," I was drawn into a relationship of implicit intimacy that my Yankee grandmother would certainly have condemned as inappropriate if not downright impertinent. To adopt the second person in my own writing would draw some innocent other into similarly suspect relations.

What I was resisting, of course, was the seduction upon which writing rests. If I admitted neither "I" nor "you," or at the most admitted "I" without "you," I could break the erotic connection or, failing that, cover it over and keep it decently from view. Only slowly, and with more distress than these essays perhaps reveal, have "I" emerged, and later "you." Now, whether I use the words or not, the beings they represent are never absent from my consciousness. "I" and "you," whispering our sweet nothings back and forth.

Here we are, then, you and I. And now? And now? . . .

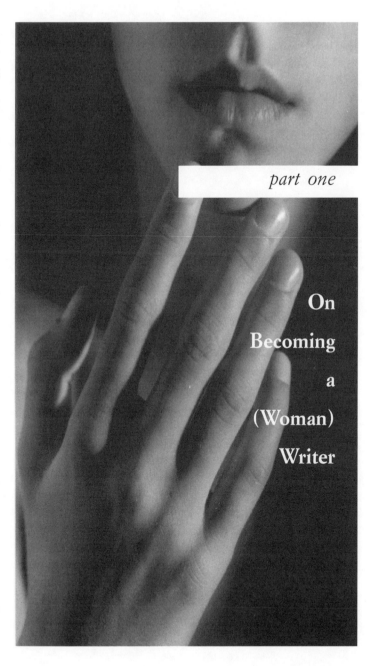

part one

On
Becoming
a
(Woman)
Writer

Voice

Lessons

1. PEAR TREES

*t*he question I am most
often asked when I
speak to students and
others interested in writing is,
How did you find your voice?
I have some trouble with this
locution because "find" always
suggests to me the discovery,
generally fortuitous, of some
lack or loss. I have found an
occasional four-leaf clover. I
have found a mate. I have,
more than once, found my
way home. But is a voice sus-
ceptible of the same sort of
revelation or retrieval? Hasn't
mine simply always been there,
from my earliest lallation to
the "I love you" I called after
my husband on his way to
school several hours ago?

But of course, I remind myself, the question doesn't concern *my* voice at all but the

voice of another woman (also named Nancy Mairs, confusingly enough) whose "utterances" are, except for the occasional public reading, literally inaudible: not, strictly speaking, a voice at اً ., but a fabrication, a device. And when I look again at the dictionary, I see that "find" can indeed also mean "devise." The voice in question, like the woman called into being to explain its existence, is an invention.

But of whom? For simplicity's sake, we assume that the voice in a work is that of the writer (in the case of nonfiction) or one invented by her (in the case of fiction). This assumption describes the relationship between writer (the woman in front of a luminous screen) and persona (whoever you hear speaking to you right now) adequately for most readers. And maybe for most writers, too. Until that earnest student in the second row waves a gnawed pencil over her head and asks, timidly as a rule because hers is the first question, "How did you find your voice?"

As though "you" were a coherent entity already existing at some original point, who had only to open her mouth and agitate her vocal chords—or, to be precise, pick up her fingers and diddle the keys—to call the world she had in mind into being. Not just a writer, an Author. But I've examined this process over and over in myself, and the direction of this authorial plot simply doesn't ring true. In the beginning, remember, was the *Word*. Not me. And the question, properly phrased, should probably be asked of my voice: How did you find (devise, invent, contrive) your Nancy?

On the day I was married (actually, a few days beforehand, since I got rather caught up in last-minute preparations), I stopped writing. These two events (one event and one nonevent, to be precise) might have been purely coincidental, but I suspect that they weren't. Although thirty years later I can see that that day marked a beginning, which, like a healthy rootstock, has burgeoned over time into beginning after beginning after beginning, I had no such sense then. On that day something came to an end, something I might call my artistic youth.

I was nineteen then, and I had been writing for at least eleven years. And I mean writing: not just dutiful school assignments, though I did plenty of those, but sheaves of poems and short stories scribbled in time stolen from school assignments—the very opposite of dutiful, downright subversive of duty. What was different about married life, I wonder, that made it resistant to subversion of this sort? Or—and I think this is the same question in different guise—what did I think writing was that my married state seemed to debar it?

The facts refute one easy explanation. My husband was not responsible for my silence. As anyone who's read Charlotte Perkins Gilman's story "The Yellow Wallpaper" will recall, some husbands, wary of the way artistic endeavor resists control, will suppress it—if not outright then by ignoring, deprecating, even ridiculing it. But George always liked my writing, and he urged me to continue it. In the years since I've established myself as a writer, we've both been happier, in part, I think, because I'm doing what we've both always believed I should be doing. So, although I tend to blame George for everything from lost teaspoons to the colonies of blue mold sprouting at the back of the refrigerator and it would be both convenient and credible to blame him for the nearly fatal consequences to my writing of its collision with marriage, I'll have to look elsewhere.

I had no explicit reason, back in 1963, to believe that a married woman could not be a writer. In fact, my aunt was one—a married woman writer, that is—although the way my grandmother referred to her daughter's poetry and her psychoanalysis in the same shuddering breath was, I'll admit unnerving. Aunt Jane aside, however, I didn't have any particular reason to believe that a married woman could— or should—write more than grocery lists and thank-you notes for the christening presents. In high school I'd had a passion for historical romances, many written by women, but as an English major in college I'd been assigned virtually no works by women, married or otherwise, so women's literary legitimacy seemed dubious. Both in classes and on my own I'd read plenty of works about women, of course. Most of these women weren't married, though they were generally trying to get that way, and the book ended when they finally made it. Those who were married seemed to have few creative options: They could knit, sometimes with powerful consequences. They could commit adultery, but then they were likely to heave themselves under the wheels of a train or gobble fistfuls of arsenic. Childbirth was all too often fatal. And if they got really out of hand, there was always the attic.

Thus, I encountered few enough figures to suggest how to function happily as a wife, much less a writing wife. But the absence of models was only one strand in an elaborate knot. Another, perhaps even more important, was spun by the need that sent me hurtling into marriage while I was still, in every way, a girl, and here both literature and psychoanalysis are again at least partially implicated. From the age of four on, I had no father. The figurative lack that some believe at once underwrites and undermines human artistic expression[1] was accompanied, in my case, by a more literal hole, a wound even, and I desired, above everything else, to stop it up. Whatever I wrote, I wrote out of that pain, and whatever I wrote assuaged the pain a little but never enough. Everything I saw and read informed me, assured me, that what I needed to fill that void was a man. Maybe it also told me what to do with him, and with our life together, after I got him, but I neglected that part. I just wanted to get him, and plug him in, and ease the pain. Since I had written entirely out of yearning and now I yearned no more, I had neither the motivation nor the material to keep on writing.

Does this sound far-fetched? Probably it does. I'm writing about "prefeminist" experience in an era that labels itself, more wistfully than accurately, "postfeminist." You'll just have to take my word for it: once I was married, nothing in my life seemed worth writing about. I was, perhaps, unusually naive. I favored the surfaces of poems by Sara Teasdale and Edna St. Vincent Millay. I'd been given the *Sonnets from the Portuguese* but never, of course, *Aurora Leigh*. Sylvia Plath was still alive on my wedding day (though not for long thereafter), but I'd never heard of her and didn't read her work for almost a decade. Anne Sexton was still alive, too, but I hadn't heard of her, either. Or of Adrienne Rich. Or of Carolyn Kizer. As a college freshman I did hear May Sarton read, my diary records, but obviously I didn't "hear" her. For some reason (not hard now to fathom, but then I didn't even wonder), the only painting by

Georgia O'Keeffe in my art text was of the Brooklyn Bridge, not the secret spaces of shells or bones or flowers. Not one work in my yearlong music course had been composed by a woman.

Maybe if I'd gone to Radcliffe or Smith, my experience would have been different, but my little women's college was playing it safe. A few of the writers and artists we studied were still alive, but they were mostly men, and what they were depicting wasn't going on in my life. Later I got a job as a technical editor, and then I read Carl Sagan on the greenhouse effect on Mars and Venus, and Ursula Marvin on the composition of moon rocks, but what they were depicting wasn't going on in my life, either—or anybody else's, for that matter. I did read *The Feminine Mystique*, and later *The Golden Notebook*, and later still *The Second Sex*, but for a long time I couldn't (or, I now see, I wouldn't, didn't dare) discern how these might be about me.

Here's what *was* going on in my life after I was married. A final year of college. A brief, unhappy stint of grade-school teaching. The birth of a daughter. A job. An episode of depression so debilitating as to require six months of confinement in a state mental hospital. After my release, the same job for another year. The birth of a son. A different job. Also weekly sessions with a psychiatrist, summer vacations in New Hampshire, season tickets to the Charles Playhouse, occasional concerts by the Chorus Pro Musica and visits to museums and to zoos, increasing involvement in the antiwar movement. Yearnings? Yes, but not the sort I knew how to articulate and none I'd have counted as art if I had been able to speak.

After about eight years, I started committing adultery,

and again at long last I had something to write about: sexual arousal masked as a troubled heart, which was more fruitful, I found, than my interminably troubled mind. The poems started coming reliably enough in number and quality to get me into graduate school. Luckily, I refrained from throwing myself under an MBTA car (the railroads being by this time pretty well defunct) and arsenic in quantity is hard to come by nowadays. All the same, adultery proved increasingly unsatisfactory. For one thing, no matter how discreetly it's handled, it's awfully hard on a marriage. And increasingly I knew myself committed to George and the children. I couldn't have both commitment and independence: not what I meant by commitment, not what I meant by independence. For his own reasons, George never forced— never even asked—me to choose. He let me travel to the point of choice on my own.

I chose him. But did I choose only him? On my wedding day I seemed to have chosen between marriage and writing, not consciously but firmly nonetheless. I believed that choice necessary, and so I suppose it was, even though now I perceive the dilemma as a false one. The choice I made nearly twenty years later—the one to remain actively married rather than frittering away my emotional energies—circumvented the dilemma by breaking my reliance on romance for inspiration. The dilemma was beside the point. I could have both marriage and writing. The price was labor, an awful lot of it: grinding, occasionally wearisome, often scary, and absolutely without end. I had to change my intellectual and aesthetic beliefs about the world and about what I was doing in it, and I had to keep on changing them as the world changed—and I changed in it—forever. The reward: well, who knew?

21

The fact is that adultery had been hard on more than my marriage. It was fixing me in amber. The golden aromatic resin was thickening. I could feel its sticky pressure in my nostrils, down my throat. I was sucked in by love and loss. I had to get out. But how? What else could rouse me to write? What else did I know? *There were the babies, and the blood, the way bread yields and sighs like flesh under your fist, the death of the little dog, so sudden, unlooked for, and the way your tears choked you as you folded him into the pillowcase and heaped dirt over the linen, and then too your body, its betrayal sudden also but its diminishment protracted so that grief, you learn, will actually never end, and the babies gone, and soon the blood as well.* These were the sorts of things I knew, or was learning, and so I tried some of them out on the guys (it was just them and me that year) in a poetry workshop. "Yech," they said.

And kept on saying. That was a bad time for me, alone with the guys, who knew what writing was because they were doing it, who knew that what I was doing, to the extent that they weren't doing it, wasn't writing, not the real thing (muscular, tough-minded, penetrating, gritty), and who didn't mind telling me so. One or another has gone on telling me so ever since. "Stop squandering your time on this feminist stuff," Edward Abbey told me for years. And after he died, a reviewer for the *New York Times* caught up the tune before it faded away: "a waste of a 'talented voice,'" he wrote. I don't think any man has ever suggested I give up writing. It's just that a lot of them want me to write something *else*. (My mother does too, by the way, so I'm using the word *man* pretty loosely.)

Whether some of us like it or not, men (in the loose sense

of the word) have determined and continue to dominate our culture, and that still (though who knows for how long) includes the arts. It's been men senators ranting about queer photographers and crucifixes in piss and the need to protect the taxpayers' hard-earned pennies from being squandered on obscenities (environmental degradation and the deaths of people with brown or red or yellow or black skin being something other than obscene). It was a man director of the National Endowment for the Arts who, lashed by the senators' tongues, scurried around demanding pledges of sanitation before doling out his meager funds. Women (white heterosexual middle-class educated ones, anyway) may more frequently succeed at grabbing men's goodies— the directorship of the National Endowment for the Arts among them—and call themselves postfeminist when they do, but these are still men's goodies and will be as long as men determine what they are, what you must believe and do in order to get them, and what they're worth.

As the feminist theologian Rosemary Radford Ruether points out, "It is almost impossible for an individual alone to dissent from this culture. Alternative cultures and communities must be built up to support the dissenting consciousness."[2] If I'd been trapped forever by some evil genie in that poetry workshop with all those guys doing the polite equivalent of sticking their fingers down their throats in response to my writing, I can't imagine what would have become of me, but it might have warranted my enshrinement as the tragic heroine of some "real" work of art, along the lines of Hedda Gabler, maybe, or Blanche DuBois. As luck would have it, however, I found myself in another poetry workshop altogether, gathered under the pear trees

23

outside a very old farmhouse in New Hampshire on summer Mondays, listening to, reflecting upon, discussing, and celebrating the poems of a small but diverse group of women.

And when (around the time I began my doctoral work) my poems began to turn to essays about a woman's life, the life of a woman's body, the life of a crippled woman's body, no one at Skimmilk Farm moved to banish me from the Monday workshop. In the ivory phallus, I had found, where poets hardly speak even to fiction writers (let alone to essayists, literary critics, and the like), the genres are like armed camps, and transgressing their boundaries can result in swift expulsion. If I'd started reading an essay in my poetry workshop there, I'd have been cut off and told to register for the nonfiction workshop meeting down the hall. At the Farm, the women simply listened to my essays very hard and laughed in all the right places. Although I have not seen many of them for years now, I still think of them as my audience. They, and all the others like them whom I've never met, are the ones I write for.

And really, what more can we—as writers, as artists, as human beings—do for one another? In the middle of a sentence I'm having trouble with, when my attention strays and I find myself cringing in anticipation of the next inevitable *yech* (and I do cringe; old habits die hard), I say: Let the masters of the written word cling to their bodiless principles. Let them pronounce what is interesting and what is not, what is a poem and what is not, what merits their grudging praise and what does not. For myself, I want another model. I want to hear *this* poem by *this* person on *this* muggy August morning under the pear trees. I want to

24

know what it is doing in the life of her work, and in my life as well. I want to give her the courage to say the next hard thing, without fear of ridicule or expulsion if she strays across the borders of good taste, good sense, or good judgment demarcated by a tradition she has had no part in forming. I want her to do the same for me.

This is what we can *all* do to nourish and strengthen one another: listen to one another very hard, ask hard questions, too, send one another away to work again, and laugh in all the right places.

2. THE GROVES OF ACADEME

In fact, the autobiographical pitch and timbre distinguishing this voice that utters me developed unconsciously but not spontaneously during the years after finding community under the pear trees, when, as a doctoral student, I began at last to attend seriously to the words and intonations of women as women. I found my writing voice, and go on finding it, in precisely the same way that I came to my first utterances: by listening to the voices around me, imitating them, then piping up on my own—timidly at first, making plenty of mistakes, being corrected, correcting myself, listening some more. . . .

Up until this point, my writing had been rooted in fertile but decidedly uneven emotional ground, and now I began to tap intellectual sources instead. No, that implicit split between ardor and intellect is the very opposite of what I mean: ideas now erupted into and became indistinguishable from my emotional and even my corporeal life. I could feel them in my flesh, quickening my breath, itching my fingers, spilling out through the nib of the black Parker fountain pen my husband gave me as an anniversary present appropriate to a writing wife. I can trace this development—as I entered, inhabited, and then slipped out of the academy— from my earliest attempts at articulating a deliberately, if sometimes falteringly, feminist vision onward: a kind of archaeology of voice.

By the time I established myself as a doctoral student in English literature with a particular interest in works by women, I was pushing forty. I'm no longer sure why I started to work on a doctorate—and probably never was. I certainly didn't burn with ambition either to "get" or to "be" a Ph.D. I'd come to like the classroom, however, and the Catholic high school where I'd been teaching after I finished my M.F.A. fired me. I lacked credentials for the public schools, which I could acquire while I worked on a Ph.D. in English education, teaching freshman composition in the bargain. The fact that I happen to like teaching freshman composition, both because I believe it to be the most important course in the university curriculum and because I feel an inarticulate passion for the mute helplessness of freshmen, signaled my unsuitability for doctoral work (no true scholar would so abase himself), but fortunately no one took it seriously.

By 1979, I'd completed the course work for a Ph.D. in English education, all but the required course in advanced sadistics. Then, after a summer of those workshops at Skimmilk Farm, where I also devoured a shelf of books by Virginia Woolf, I returned to Tucson with permission to speak.

I came to feminism in my characteristic fashion—late. Trailing a good decade or more behind the vanguard of feminist scholars, I discovered women writers and began writing a woman's life myself. While other women had been, rumor had it, burning their bras, I was still strapping myself into mine, even though my breasts are so small that it routinely rode up and threatened to strangle me. Arriving in Tucson on an August morning when the temperature was a hundred three in the shade, I stripped it off. (My conversions, like all my acts, are experientially rather than theoretically grounded. I didn't object to my bra on principle; I just couldn't stand the grip of wet elastic around my neck.)

Similarly, although I wasn't entirely unaware of feminist issues, I could never quite see how they applied to my life and, thus, why I should act on them. And in truth, for a number of reasons, they may have impinged on me less than on some others. I had spent my formative years in a household of self-sufficient women: my grandmother, divorced long before my birth, supported herself as a bank teller, and my widowed mother worked as a school secretary until her remarriage when I was eleven. I attended a college where even in those prefeminist days female competence was taken for granted under the stage lights, in the chemistry lab, on the hockey field, and definitely at the bridge table. My husband took part in running our household and rearing our children without the fuss and fanfare that many men make to call attention, like toddlers assisting Mommy, to their "helpfulness."

Small wonder, perhaps, that such privileged circumstances had obscured other women's pain, not to mention my own. For I had been, in spite of my good fortune, inexplicably and often bitterly unhappy for reasons that feminist readings of my experience were at last enabling me to scrutinize and then even to manage. In the spring semester of 1980, I entered my first explicitly feminist gathering; a graduate seminar entitled "Woman As Sign."

The setting turned out to be extraordinary because the professor, having lost one baby and in danger of losing another, was put to bed just a week or so into the semester, and instead of canceling the course or turning it over to someone else, she moved it to her home. Every week, then, in place of the plastic and fluorescence to which we'd grown inured, we gathered in an airy space around Susan's couch: a dozen or so women, one (rather brave, as I think on it) man, and Alden, humping up higher and rounder each week, her mute presence bespeaking the knowledges our books and seminar papers refused us until, just a couple of weeks before the semester's end, she showed up in tiny but thriving person to set a kind of seal on the proceedings.

In this company, embarrassed by my stunted growth, wary, curious, and curiously afraid, I began to learn to read again and to try my hand at formal feminist criticism, straining after a tone of subtle irony. (Subtlety struck me as a great virtue in those days: I didn't want to mark myself as ingenuous by explaining some point that everyone who knew anything took for granted. But I couldn't figure out just what "everyone" knew, except that it was obviously more than I did. I still can't, and it still is, but I forgive myself for bafflement more readily now.) This voice—arch and insiderly—was not my own.

In the same semester that the "Woman As Sign" seminar awaited Alden Carroll's arrival, a departure yanked me into another opportunity for growth. I admire people who leap into larger selves with the élan of sky divers entering the ether, but I grow only if yanked, I'm afraid, and then only under protest. In this case, my reluctance was born as much of sadness as of timidity. I had known and admired Sally Perper for eight years, since first coming to the University of Arizona, and when pancreatic cancer forced her to give up teaching just days before the spring 1980 semester began, I assumed her "Composition Through Literature" without the joy I'd have felt otherwise at being permitted to teach the course.

Today I remember with pleasure every detail about that class except for a model I wrote to prepare my students for their major assignment, a documented essay about a literary work of their own choosing. The structure of my piece was clear, the ideas were accessible, and the mechanics of documentation were correct, but the tone was all wrong, designed to baffle and discomfit the ordinary reader. Bafflement and discomfiture are much of the point, if not quite the whole to it, in the academy. The Haves and Have Nots of general society are paralleled there by the Knows and Know Nots. The same principle of exclusion operates, but on a linguistic rather than a material basis. To belong you need a word hoard, as the Anglo-Saxons would say: linguistic currency, in both senses of the phrase. Unfortunately, thanks to inflation, deflation, and the frequent replacement of one monetary system by another—now cowry shells, now coins, now Coleman lanterns—it can be pretty hard to figure out your worth. My use of words like "mythopoetic" obviously reflected considerable anxiety about my position. Not that "mythopoetic" isn't a perfectly good word. Not

29

that I wouldn't still use it if I needed it. Just that the nature of that need has changed, and I would no longer risk replicating that earlier, edgy, spurious need in my students.

Not until my preliminary doctoral examination did I begin, by treating literary insight as a variety of personal experience, to hear a voice I might "own," although the emotional din of that occasion threatened to drown out those peepings. The fact that shifting to the Ph.D. program in English literature prolonged my course of study had suited me. I was a happy student, a happy teacher, and, thanks to the chronic progressive nature of my multiple sclerosis, I was almost wholly without professional purpose. The future for which my classmates were preparing themselves diligently, yearningly—freedom from freshmen, publication in *PMLA*, sabbaticals at the Bodleian or in Tuscany, promotion to a full professorship, maybe even an endowed chair—was closing to me. Why hurry toward my own obscurer fate? The university had anticipated hangers-on, however, with a system of regulations designed to purge itself automatically of such indigestible bits if they failed to eliminate themselves voluntarily. My end was in view.

That it couldn't be reached except by examination isn't surprising, given that an academic degree attests to capabilities, one might even say powers, jealously guarded by those who possess them already. The difference between an academic degree and a driver's license, say, or a medical technician's certificate is that at least some academic powers may have no practical consequences, may not even manifest themselves in any quantifiable manner, and so may seem mysterious, elusive, ineffable, transcendent—an awful lot like God's. Testing godlikeness—as opposed to determining whether a person understands the meaning of an octagonal road sign or can slip a needle neatly into a vein—can be a bit tricky: the results tend to be so mixed. But preliminary doctoral examinations purport to do so.

I did not understand then, and I still do not, what of value this system was believed to reveal. Memory? If a Ph.D. attests to the holder's capacity to retain and retrieve information without resorting to sources, then I oughtn't to have one. I can't even remember how to spell "weird" without looking it up, much less retrace Leopold Bloom's progress through Dublin—or even Clarissa Dalloway's through London, to which I feel far closer—without returning to *Ulysses* or *Mrs. Dalloway*. If not memory, perhaps writing skill? But no matter how substantial, clearly organized, and charmingly expressed a little essay I might whip up in three hours, I would always, always do better in, say, three days, and I suspect everyone else would, too. Grace under pressure? This could indeed be a valuable quality in some circumstances, but not those likely to be encountered by a professor of literature, who can always say, if asked a question he can't answer, "I don't know. Give me a day or so to think about it."

I once heard a professor, challenged by a group of graduate students to defend the examination system, blurt, "Well, I had to go through it, and so should you." There's the real reason, I suspect. Examinations visit the misery of one generation on the next—the scholarly equivalent of hazing. They invite students to exhibit work that, produced under adverse circumstances involving anxiety, lack of resources, limited time, and mental and physical exhaustion, falls short of their best, and they force students to accept judgments based on that hastily conceived and frantically scribbled or uttered work. Meditation, reflection, revision—the essential elements of solid intellectual production—are deliberately debarred.

I remember walking out of my oral prelims to find my husband waiting, a bottle of Drambuie hidden in a paper bag for a toast.

"How did it go?" he asked.

"I passed!" I told him, and burst into tears. As a younger woman, I'd believed that opening oneself up to experience—all experience—offered the greatest opportunity for intellectual and spiritual growth. Now, suddenly, I saw that there are some experiences one simply ought never to have, and prelims constituted such an experience for me. Over time, my humiliation—my sense of having been required to present myself in a compromised light I would never have chosen, any more than I'd have chosen to strip my misshapen body to its skin, even less—faded, of course. But a sliver of grief remains lodged near my heart.

I was surprised, then, rereading years later the essays written for the exam, that their tone hardly sounds bleak or distressed. On the contrary, the voice is breathless with excitement, with exertion, with laughter, but not with anxiety. This woman sounds like she's having as good a time as I always do when the world drops away and I am left alone with language. Listening to her, I am carried back to a little room with one high window where I hunch intently at a grey metal desk under fluorescent flicker, sucking at cigarettes and red cans of Coke, pushing my fountain pen across sheet after sheet of yellow legal-size paper . . . and sure enough, I'm having a wonderful time.

"Self. Life. Writing. Self-life-writing. Selflifewriting," the first essay of my prelims began.

"Autobiography. . . . a particular kind of writing, writing about a real life, one that really (maybe) happened (when?). . . . At once easier and harder to write than biography—easier because the writer doesn't have to do a whole lot of research, except in the archives of memory, which stay open longer hours than many of us would wish, and because she's automatically an authority, whose mistakes (if she's caught) will be forgiven as slips of memory, not excoriated as sloppy research, and because, as at once the writer and the subject, she doesn't risk the confusion of identity biographers sometimes experience; harder because. . . . Well, think of the pain; think of the responsibility.

Out of this half-humorous tumble of words rang my own voice. Not romantic anguish, not guy talk, not muteness or critical bombast masking intellectual cowardice, though I had learned from trying on each of those rejected styles. I would speak plainly out of my own experience, to an audience I liked and trusted, about a woman's life, making it up as I went along. I was on my way to nowhere in particular and in no hurry to get there. I would poke into the byways, much as George and I would later meander through the Cotswolds despite the tuts and stifled groans of my stepfather in the rear seat, for whom getting lost clearly did not constitute a lark. I would take my time. I would sometimes feel pained and burdened by the processes of self-creation/-discovery/-revelation, but I would also laugh out loud more than I could have anticipated, and others, weeping and laughing along with me, would provide consolation. I might *work* alone but I would never *be* alone, not as long as I could call out and muse on a response. "I" would be I.

My reward, such as it might be: my voice's Nancy.

Body

at

Work

*b*y the time I reached
the end of my doc-
toral studies in 1984,
I was well on my way to another life. My "good girl"
voice was beginning to break
up. I was laughing too hard to
control it consistently. I was
beginning to have too good a
time. My sense of release must
have been, in part, simply a
function of age. Over forty, I
knew that I had let the time
for establishing myself as a
reputable academic slip past. I
no longer wanted to do so. I
don't think I ever really had.
When a brilliant young Ameri-
canist I knew touted the ne-
cessity for "intellectual rigor,"
instead of leaping to uphold
the standard he'd erected I
heard "*mortis*" and shuddered.
Physically. As though trying to

keep my joints limber, my muscles loose. My body balked at the fringe of the sacred groves surrounding the foot of the pale tower and refused to enter their cool dappled shade. If I were going thus to exile myself, then the conventions of academic discourse couldn't serve me.

I wasn't just growing old, of course. I was growing, well, odd. I was reading feminist theory, especially French feminist theory, and testing theoretical insights against my own experience by writing personal essays. I had begun at last—as surely one ought by forty—to develop a feel for my own work. In this spirit—the spirit of having something to do and being eager to get on with it—I put together my doctoral dissertation.

Conceiving a dissertation under these circumstances was problematic, of course. In the English department at my university, a dissertation was supposed to entail the study of someone else's literary work, and of what other scholars had already said about that work, rather than the production of new literature. I had prepared myself most thoroughly as a student of Virginia Woolf, but terrific feminist scholarship was already pouring out of established academics, like Jane Marcus and Louise DeSalvo, with access to more current sources than my library possessed. I didn't relish the idea of picking and poking at Woolf's corpus to find some tiny patch, untouched probably because it had been rejected rather than overlooked, for ritual scrutiny. I didn't want to be dutiful.

Luckily, some adventurous young scholars in the department agreed to form my dissertation committee, and the idea of an "original literary dissertation," in the form of a series of feminist autobiographical essays, appealed to them.

Theirs were real ears for me to address, and their responses gave me a sense that whatever I wrote was embedded in an ongoing dialogue. The intellectual work they demanded has served me well. My essays were amply furnished with auto-biographical scenes of marriage, sex, childrearing, chronic physical and emotional illness, and similarly intimate subjects, but without a theoretical frame these remained purely private concerns. Compelled by my committee to clarify what I think I'm doing each time I sit down to strive, through language, to make the world make sense, I envisioned at last the aim that has underlain my work thereafter: to nullify the splitting—of body from spirit, of critic from creator, of intellect from desire, of self from other—characteristic of Western discourse, a process rooted in the division of a multi-various humanity into two hierarchized genders. From this point on, a critical consciousness about gender and language has informed my literary voice.

The ideas I found in the university—ideas that, ironi-cally, led me away from the university—effected an intel-lectual liberation as powerful as the literary one I experienced by finding a widening audience for my work at Skimmilk Farm, at the Bread Loaf Writers' Conference, through public readings, in small literary reviews. The two "liberations" are linked in an important way: both revealed to me the extent to which I was writing about the body. Although ideas about language and the body are common currency among feminist academics, they offer liberating possibilities for all kinds of writers, so here's the story I've pieced together from them and what it's done to and for me.

From the moment of birth, at every level, human beings who are more alike than different become polarized into two absolutely exclusive classes with very different and ill-distributed symbolic powers. Psychoanalysis famously organizes the polarity of human beings into male and female around the having or not having of the phallus. Now, the phallus is not just "the little thingummy that Freud talks about," psychoanalyst Jacques Lacan promises,[1] but the concept starts with that little thingummy all the same. As Susan Hardy Aiken points out, "By continuing to use the term *phallus* even while insisting that *phallus* and *penis* are not synonyms, Lacan is of course nonetheless privileging male physical difference, since *phallus* and *penis* are semantically equivalent—or at least they once were (pre-Freud and pre-Lacan)"[2]—and attach to only half the members of the human population. After all, in this scheme one has or does not have, might lose or has already lost or can never lose, something of supreme worth . . . to whom? What intrinsic value, from a woman's point of view, does a whatever-it-is have, beyond its decorative function and its potential for putting out very small fires? She can not imagine the pleasures it affords the bearer, nor does she need to as long as she can rub her own thighs together. She's not likely to covet every protuberance she sees—a wart on the nose, for instance, or a goiter. And to add to her self-sufficiency/-satisfaction, she can follow up the pleasures of the sexual act not just by another sexual act, and another, but by a full replication of the human form through which human experience continues to contribute to the construct "humanity."

Nevertheless, if to have a penis is better than not to have one (and Freudian theory rests on this assumption), then he who has a penis is superior to she who does not, and male dominance becomes a matter of biological course. But naturally the matter is not so simple, because we do not dominate that to which we feel simply and clearly superior. Like as not we ignore it, or at most feed it a dish of kibbles every night. The male human being hardly ignores the female. On the contrary, he constructs out of a few inches of flesh which he has got and she hasn't a monument to difference of staggering dimensions, to whose rule woman is subjected—thrown under—in an act of violence all out of proportion for a being who possesses that which, by its very attachment to the base of his trunk, marks his privilege. Unless the mark isn't so very clear. Unless she's got something he hasn't got, she who is all smooth down there, except for that little slit which, pried open, reveals fold after ruffled fold like dense pink draperies shrouding—what? What has she got down there? What is she hiding? Ah, it is . . . a baby!

"Balls!" he rumbles. "Who'd want to make a thing like that, all noise and stink and only half finished?" And off he stomps to create "relatively lasting, eternal, transcendental objects, while the woman creates only perishables—human beings."[3] But what, the woman ponders, watching his broad retreating back, is more perishable about a human being than about an artifact? The human being will die and can be killed, of course, but so can a poem be burned, a painting slashed, a cathedral crumbled by an earthquake. Leaving aside the construct of an imperishable human soul, the fact remains that the human being possesses a capacity beyond that of any technical/symbolic creation: the engendering of another human being with the same capacity, a link in the chain that signifies eternal life.

The male, no matter how many ejaculations he has into

how many vaginas, will never *himself* bring forth such a link, will never *in this way* be part of the procreative chain, and so he erects the phallus as a substitute for the baby he can never bear. No wonder, then, that the phallus appears as an instrument of force. He will use it to kidnap the baby, to co-opt it into his own chain, and to erase any taint of the mother who made it by relegating her to the space between links, where she can give no tongue to her primary right, can never accuse the thief.

I am not talking about the baby as a cute cooing bundle in a blue blanket, any more than Lacan is talking about the phallus as a thingummy. I am not conjuring up an image of a father snatching up the infant ascribed to him and running with it through the hospital corridors, through the streets, dodging the police and the FBI as it wails and wets on him and roots at his chest. I am only saying that there must be something the man wants terribly, unbearably, if he's willing to use all the force in the world to grab it, and I don't think it can be something he possesses already (even if he's afraid of losing it). The phallus itself is simply not enough to bring about its own erection as a weapon of war, of annihilation. Something more must be at stake, something infinitely precious, something that can lift him above his own inevitable death and make him part of a transcendent creation as no artifact, no matter how brilliant, no matter how beautiful, can do: his creation can only stand in for the baby.

Which may or may not be his. The poems are his, he knows. He watched them flow out of the tip of his pen and stain the blank sheet permanently. The paintings are his. But the baby? Who's to say whether the baby is his? Only the mother, and only if she chooses to name him. What kind of a guarantee is that? What if she's lying? He must have some means of legitimating his claim, of snatching the baby and marking it his. She needs no such thing: she was there when it went in and there when it came out, regardless of who put it there. What is hers by right he must take by force, through law, by giving it Lacan's Name-of-the-Father: "the patronym, patriarchal law, patriarchal identity, language as our inscription into patriarchy. The Name-of-the-Father is the fact of the attribution of paternity by law, by language."[4] With his own tongue the father has named the baby. Now it is his.

And yet he can't rest easy in his possession of the baby. What has been snatched by force might always be reclaimed by force. Thus, he must legitimate not only his claim to the baby but also his means of getting the baby in the first place. He has only the mother's word that the baby is his at all, and "any suspicion of the mother's fidelity betrays the Name-of-the-Father as the arbitrary imposition it is."[5] He had better put the mother beyond reproach, then, by possessing her as well. So he marries her and gives her the Name-of-the-Father, too. But all is still not well. She has, for one thing, this boundless eroticism, this wriggling delight in being touched all over (she can come while he's sucking her nipple, for God's sake, as though the thingummy weren't even there), what the French call her *jouissance*, "a kind of potlatch in the world of orgasms, a giving, expending, dispensing of pleasure without concern about ends or closure"[6]; and she doesn't seem to distinguish him from any other lover or to care much whether she gets a baby or not. If he is to own her, he must confine her through an elaborate system of locked doors and taboos, keep her away from other men, focus her attention down there where the babies go in and come out, make her forget everything but the babies.

Once he gets her settled into domesticity, however, and gets a baby, the baby seems to belong to her, not him. They are forever together, nuzzling each other, rocking and humming and babbling. This doesn't much matter if it's a girl baby, since some stranger will one day get his own baby out of her; but it it's a boy baby, it's of his line, and he must wrest it away from its tricky mother and insert it into the chain of immortality he is forging. "No," he bellows, louder than Rumpelstiltskin, at the cowering mother with the cowering child behind her skirts. "You can't have this one. This one is mine. He is my *son*." And named by the father, the child becomes a man.

In order to get what he wants, then, the father must must have power to coerce those around him to meet his demands. To have power is to alienate oneself, however, because power is always power *over*, and the preposition demands an object. The fundamental structure of patriarchy is thus binary: me/not me, active/passive, culture/nature, normal/deviant, good/bad, masculine/feminine, public/private, political/personal, form/content, subjective/objective, friend/enemy, true/false. . . . It is a structure, both spatial and temporal, predicated upon separation, not relation. It demands rupture, the split into halves engendered by the abrupt erection of the phallus: those who have and those who have not. It speaks the language of opposites.

Which is not women's language, since women, for a variety of reasons, live in a polymorphic rather than a dimorphic world, a world in which the differentiation of self from other may never completely take place, in which multiple selves may engage multiply with the multiple desires of the creatures in it. Some theorists would claim that all subjects function thus. But as Julia Kristeva points out, female subjectivity, traditionally linked to cyclical and monumental time rather than to linear time, lies outside "language considered as the enunciation of sentences (noun + verb, topic–comment, beginning–ending)." Possessing an "irreducible identity, without equal in the opposite sex and, as such, exploded, plural, fluid," a woman may be driven "to break the code, to shatter language, to find a specific discourse closer to the body and the emotions, to the unnameable repressed by the social contract."[7]

The difference that emerges here is not the polarity intrinsic in the dominant discourse, which reduces "woman to man's opposite, *his* other, the negative of the positive."[8] No, this is an absolute and radical alterity that enfolds the other, as in pregnancy a woman's immune system shuts down in such a way that she shelters and nourishes, rather than rejects and expels, the foreign body within her: "Cells fuse, split, and proliferate; volumes grow, tissues stretch, and body fluids change rhythm, speeding up or slowing down. Within the body, growing as a graft, indomitable, there is an other. And no one is present, within that simultaneously dual and alien space, to signify what is going on."[9] Feminine discourse is not the language of opposites but a babel of eroticism, attachment, and empathy.

The binary mode of structuring the world is agonistic, to use the term employed by Walter J. Ong, who associates it with the adversarial nature of male ceremonial combat and contrasts it with the irenic, or conciliatory, discourse characteristic of "women's liberation movements, student demonstrations, pacifism, and the substitution of the existential, noncontesting fugitive hero . . . in place of the agonistic hero of the older epic and romance."[10] The discrepancy between these two modes of being in the world has manifold, often violent, consequences, of which one has affected me most deeply: *agon* (contest or conflict) in the academy.

"*Ludus*," notes Ong, "the Latin word for school, we have seen means also war games." One cannot go to school, it seems, without going to war, where women, Virginia Woolf and Julia Kristeva and Carol Gilligan and myriad other feminist writers tell us, do not wish to be. Thus, as Ong says, "the agonistic elements in academia are entangled with the dialectic of masculine and feminine"[11]; and by tracing influences from the Renaissance to the Romantic age to coeducation and the women's liberation movement, he attests to the feminizing of academia. Perhaps, I say. But s-l-o-w-l-y. In order to earn a Ph.D., I was still required to submit a dissertation (which by definition takes apart that which has been joined together, though it is fortunately also defined as a discourse, a running back and forth: my dissertation, a collection of essays called *Plaintext*, ran back and forth a lot). I still had to defend it (to ward off its attackers) even though I think that its indefensibility may have been its one great strength. I went along. Having been in the academy for more than thirty years, I am not innocent (neither unharmed nor harmless).

But here's where intellectual liberation comes in: in the arena of the university, I was able to use the ideas I found there—the ones I've described—to lead myself out and to transform my life as a writer. I took on the dichotomies, in particular the one that has proved most vexatious to my work, the one between "creative" and "critical" writing. It is rooted, like most binary distinctions, in a very complicated struggle the crudest and most pragmatic feature of which—in this day of inflation, budget crunches, and shrinking enrollments in the humanities—is the competition for students, though the combatants tend to cast it in loftier terms.[12] I've been thus contested for, spending several years as a creative writing student (suspect because of my extensive work in Old English and Old Norse) and several more as a literature student (during which time no one in the creative writing program ever spoke to me). I've sat in workshops through endless discussions of technique, as though one were accountable for nothing one said as long as one got the tenses in the flashbacks right. I've sat in seminars through lectures on bodiless beauty and truth and art and the difference, if any, between subject and object. I've listened to and been the object of the epithets hurled from camp to camp: "Critics are out to destroy the integrity of literature." "Creative writers are intellectual slobs who take the easy way out." I've chosen, or been chosen, to be a poet–scholar in an age when that option renders me a shady character in both camps. I've become everybody's other. A true woman.

I believe in the reality of work. Period. I do not distinguish between creative and critical writing because all writing is creative. There is a pen filled with black ink. There is a blank sheet of paper. Whatever the product— poem, story, essay, letter to lover, technical report—the problem is the same: the page is empty and will have to be filled. Out of nothing, something. And all writing is critical, requiring the same sifting, selection, scrutiny, and judgment of the material at hand. The distinctions are not useful, except to people who want to engender an other with whom they can struggle and over whom they can gain power. And because they are useful in that way, they are dangerous. I prefer not to dwell in their shade.

Doctorate in hand (at least, I think it's around here somewhere), I left the academy. I don't mean that I never set foot again in its corridors and classrooms, because I certainly did, and do still off and on, as both a student and a teacher. Maybe I mean that the academy left me, worked its way out of my system or sloughed away in patches like lizard's skin. One way or another, we're not together—not in the same way—anymore.

My first sense of this shift apart (thunder)struck me one afternoon a few months after graduation, when I was rereading some material on feminine sexuality by Jacques Lacan. I'd never been able to make head or tail of the stuff, and I still couldn't. Since I really was working very hard (on the dubious principle, inculcated through years of schooling, that a halfway intelligent person can understand anything if she just puts her mind to it), I grew increasingly anxious as I struggled to decipher statements like, "The phallus is the privileged signifier of that mark where the share of the logos is wedded to the advent of desire."[13] And then it came to me: I could now afford to be stupid. No one would ever again quiz me on my "command" of Jacques Lacan. I need never grasp him again, unless out of my own desire. Professors and their examinations want all mysteries unraveled, revealed, resolved. *Ended*. Jacques Lacan and I will never end.

Once I had left the academy, I was out of it, at least from its point of view, according to which one can be only in or out. I didn't leave for lofty reasons. Under other circumstances, I might have stayed. In part I recoiled, startled by some of the behaviors I discovered would be required of me, and the force of that movement flung me to one side. In part I removed myself by degenerating physically. This gradual detachment from conventionally constructed human institutions is hard to describe. From my wheelchair, nothing looks the same. I occupy a world at the height of your navel; there is a world down there. Everything you say to one another goes over my head. Thanks to these slants in my vision, I have learned to live elsewhere.

I felt this (dis)location sharply one recent summer when I attended the School of Criticism and Theory at Dartmouth. Now, the fact that I have left the academy does not mean that I repudiate it. On the contrary, repudiation would necessitate a relationship to it which I don't perceive myself to have. But, as I said before, "it" perceives itself to have such a relationship to me. Hence this cocktail-party conversation:

> HANDSOME WOMAN OF INDETERMINATE AGE IN A POSITION OF AMBIGUOUS POWER: And what do *you* do?
>
> NANCY: I'm a writer.
>
> HWIAPAP: What do you write?
>
> NANCY: Essays, mostly. Poetry, too.
>
> HWIAPAP: Oh. A *creative* writer. (Lips close firmly around a swallow of white wine, then part again but only slightly.) What are you doing *here*?

What, indeed? I could have told her I'd come to (1) try to seduce her husband into my narrow dormitory cot, (2) retool my retrograde brain for poststructuralist, postfeminist, relativist, neohistoricist patterns of analysis, (3) study with Julia Kristeva. She'd have believed the first; the third was true, but Kristeva never arrived; the second is roughly what happened (nothing ever happens to my brain except roughly). As it was, I said none of these. She turned her face in one direction, I turned mine in another, and someone else promptly asked me the same question.

The penalty I had to pay for stepping outside the ivied walls, my experience at Dartmouth taught me, was to have the iron gates slammed behind me. I was probably the only person who saw those six weeks of study as both perfectly useless and perfectly meaningless (I didn't need a job, I didn't need references, I didn't need tenure, I didn't need to establish or enhance my reputation), but I may well have enjoyed myself the most of anyone. By living neither inside nor outside but beside the academy, I can turn to it as a source not of power but of play . . . pure pleasure . . . *jouissance* . . . the loveliest legacy of all my (mis)readings of French psychoanalytic theory. Even its pronunciation suggests the untranslatable pleasure of this word: the lips pout and then stretch, the sound slips back from the tongue's tip to be swallowed with a sigh. A word that happens to the body: writing.

In the course of writing elsewhere, shaken ever more profoundly by *jouissance* as time went by, I achieved an insight—no, that suggests too much penetrating a gaze—an intuition, let's say, that had been eluding me since I first came upon the phrase *l'écriture féminine* in French feminist theory. Such perceptions tend to come (if they come at all) latish in the game, as Shoshana Felman notes:

> Reading is an access route to discovery. But the significance of the discovery appears only in retrospect, because insight is never purely cognitive; it is to some extent always performative (*incorporated* in an act, a doing) and to that extent precisely it is not transparent to itself [my italics]. . . . And since there can never be a simultaneous, full coincidence between practice and awareness, what one understands in doing and through doing appears in retrospect: *nachträglich, après coup.*"[14]

A "feminine text," all my reading had taught me, can be produced (by a woman or a man) only through "writing the body," the "feminine" body, which is, by definition, repressed by the "phallogocentricity" of language. So far, so good. But if language systematically represses "the feminine," yet writing requires language, then what on earth would "writing the body" entail? How could one "do" it? What would it "look" like if it were done? The rational (that is, linguistically permissible) answer is something like: Nothing at all. If the feminine is the pre-symbolic, the unconscious, the repressed, then the feminine is silence.

And yet. And yet. I have a voice—a "real" voice, the one you'll hear if you call me on the telephone—which emanates from a body—a "real" body, you believe, even when you cannot see it—and which I experience as uttering a feminine existence insofar as I am aware of being a woman (which is really quite far, almost all the way). Am I doing it, then? Am I speaking the body? And if I write down my utterances, will I then be writing the body? Have I "got it" at last?

While I was stumbling around in my head like this, straining to catch faint echoes of "difference" yet privately convinced that I'd be too stupid to recognize it even if it blatted like a tuba straight into my ear, I kept myself busy at whatever writing tasks came my way. More and more often, what I wrote had bodies in it—my own body, sometimes crippled and sometimes not (the way it continues to occupy my dreams), and the bodies of others, Virginia Woolf and Alice Walker and Chinese women with bound feet—and after a while it came to me that I was writing *about* bodies because a body was writing: me. Incorporation is an act. The body writing: writing the body. I couldn't *think* such a thing, I could only *do* it.

After that, I stopped worrying about whether the feminine can or cannot be written. (I think, on balance, that it can but that reviewers won't like it much.) I just keep inscribing the fathers' words with my woman's fingers and hope that the feminine will bleed through. What has come to concern me more is the specificity that bodily existence confers. I have lost, or at least I have tried to lose, the desire that underlay my early, academic writing—the desire to establish myself as an authoritative impersonal consciousness capable of generally valid insights drawn with the humanistic equivalent of scientific objectivity. Henceforth, knowing myself incapable of touching without transforming, I must be careful in a way I never dreamed before. I can never write as Authority, as Essayist, as Literary Critic. I can write only from this body as it is now: female, white, well-educated, moderately prosperous, crippled, a Roman Catholic convert, heterosexual. . . .

This is the body who works here.

part two

Writer

As

Reader

Writing (Into) Life: Virginia Woolf and Doris Lessing

*t*he year I turned thirty-six, having all but completed the course work for a doctorate in English education with a view to devoting the rest of my professional life to teaching teachers to teach, I began to fathom that I really would have to change my life. This was not, on the surface, a new or sudden insight. From the time of my earliest extant diary, begun when I was thirteen, I have a record of periodic paroxysms of disgust with the mundanity of my existence and with my failure to accomplish anything remarkable within its miserable confines. Interestingly (I note from this distance as I could not have done then), this convulsive self-loathing was almost invariably triggered by something I was currently reading. Books assured me, in ways no other source—not films or friends or psychotherapists or priests—could do, that life could unfold otherwise; and in response to them I would yearn anew toward transformations of generally the most impractical kind.

The summer I turned seventeen, for example, at emotional loose ends between high school and college, I plunged, with anguish heightened by "half-knowledge, half-understanding, half-truth," deep into Ayn Rand's *Atlas Shrugged* and *The Fountainhead*, doubtless two of the most exquisitely adolescent of fictions, which produced in me a "desire to create" so intense and so thwarted by my circumstances that from time to time "I thought I was dying or going insane," as my diary tells me. A good many years later, after rereading an even more exotic fantasy, *The Einstein Intersection* by Samuel R. Delaney, I became "aware again," for about the zillionth time since that dismal summer, "of all I'm not doing. Creating. Exploring the mysteries. Instead, I wall myself off with student papers and course work. . . . Still clinging to my sanity. Afraid to let go lest I starve to death literally—but what's happening to me figuratively? I need to go crazier."

This view of the artistic life—variously muddling creativity, craziness, enigma, and extinction—had the potential to kill me, but I didn't know that yet. It was so familiar to me, as natural as sneezing or farting; it was all I'd ever known; I didn't even know it was there. I certainly didn't imagine it to be a composition, as much my own as one of my poems, and nothing in my reading or in my life—certainly not Ayn Rand or Samuel Delaney—had yet taught me that if I didn't like one life structure I ought to devise another. That is, until Virginia Woolf and I shared a bedroom the summer I turned thirty-six.

54

It was a matter of the merest chance. I had borrowed the room for the summer from my cousin Jon, and the books that he'd bought from a Vassar classmate at the end of the semester were stowed on a little set of shelves beside my bed. I'd spent my own college summers here, in my aunt and uncle's eighteenth-century farmhouse in southern New Hampshire, in order to care for my young cousins, freeing their mother to write. In the summer of 1979, I had come again, loaning my own children to their grandparents, to write myself. This I did, with painfully modest success, every morning, sitting in my borrowed room at a broad table, on it a jar that might hold three cone-flowers, a daylily the color of butter, and a couple of fern fronds covered with rows of tiny brown dots, together with my yellow legal-size pads, my black pens, my coffee and cigarettes, just like the real writer I hoped one day to be, though "one day" was taking such a disturbingly long time to arrive that I'd begun to suspect "never" was closer to the truth.

Working, I faced a wall, a perfectly non-metaphorical one papered in a small geometrical print, but I had a heavy old swivel chair that seemed to turn of itself toward the window on my left. Through sheer curtains I looked, morning after morning, across the narrow road to the stone wall massed with old-fashioned orange daylilies and to the unpopulated sheep pasture beyond, listening to the desultory buzz of a fly, to the little swifts in the stovepipe screeching each one to be fed its mosquitoes first, to the inside of my head for a phrase around which a whole poem might build. If I didn't hear the right one, nothing happened. It either came or it didn't.

Exhausted by willing my writing to come, if not by actually writing a lot, I recuperated every afternoon by reading. On fair days I took a book out under the pear trees, where I could look up from the page, across the poppies and zinnias among the vegetable in Uncle Kip's garden to the horses nibbling and cantering in the far field of the next farm. Being of puritanical stock, I permitted myself only serious reading, and I worked my way, with a kind of virtuous vigor, through Jon's texts: Whitehead and Sartre and Binswanger and Heidegger. Fortunately, I lumped the works of Virginia Woolf into the same stern category.

I had read Woolf before, of course. At sixteen I checked *Orlando* out of the public library. Bad idea. I can only think now that I must have mistaken it for an historical romance, like the ones by Anya Seton and Lawrence Schoonover and Mary Stewart which I gobbled between helpings of science fiction. Nevertheless, that puritanical streak already well developed in those days, I slogged through it in an agony of boredom and bemusement. At eighteen I read *Mrs. Dalloway*. Another bad idea, not mine this time but the professor's in my college modern fiction course. There are simply some writers for whom one is not, at any given moment, ready. When I was a child, my mother insisted that I sample detestable foods like lobster and broccoli each time they were served because one day my "tastes would mature," and she was right, dammit. The adolescent Nancy devoured Ernest Hemingway and D. H. Lawrence; William Faulkner and Virginia Woolf, like broccoli, required more time. Since I didn't understand this then, however, I'd never bothered to taste Woolf again.

This time I began with *A Writer's Diary*, a terrific idea, my connection with the scribbling Virginia immediate and intimate. "Yet I have some restless searcher in me," I copied from her journal into mine. "Why is there not a discovery in life? Something one can lay one's hands in and say 'This is it'? My depression is a harassed feeling. I'm looking: but that's not it—that's not it. What is it? And shall I die before I find it?"[1]

Oh, yes. "Always I am searching, yearning," I had scribbled into my own diary almost twenty years before reading hers. "Sometimes, vaguely, . . . flashes a glimpse of this greatness which is pure pain and pure joy. Yet I do not know what it is or where to find it," and the depression my fruitlessness caused me grew "beyond control, pushing me to the point of panic" and the desire for death. Although hospitalized for depression in 1967, I never learned much about the disorder; in 1979 I did not yet recognize that I'd been depressed almost continuously since I was thirteen; and I certainly did not know that a year later I would experience a depressive episode so severe that I would nearly die before finding whatever "it" might be. But at least I had found Virginia Woolf, who had survived this perilous exploration for fifty-nine years before being "driven by loneliness and silence from the habitable world."[2]

At the end of the summer I wrote Jon a check, packed Virginia into my footlocker, flew back to Tucson, and changed my life. Not all at once, mind you. Outwardly I remained pretty much the same: the harried wife, mother, teacher, and graduate student, increasingly crippled but not yet wholly balked by degenerative disease, who remained in her crumbling house and her crumbling marriage for reasons of both poverty and pride. But I shifted my doctoral program from English education to English literature, signed up for a seminar on Virginia Woolf, and, spurred on

57

by *A Room of One's Own* and *Three Guineas*, began an intensive study of feminist theory. The more I understood the cultural, psychological, and linguistic forces that caused my head to split at the thought of touching nib to yellow pad, the more determined I became not to succumb to migraine of the spirit.

That first encounter with Woolf, however, although it offered the consolation of kinship crucial to the transformation I sought, was not sufficient to assuage my horror of upheaval and establish the distance I needed to critique and then restructure the way I lived as a woman and as a writer. I was too swallowed up in my life to see it whole. Here literature proved its power, not just as the means of escape or the source of invigoration it had always been, but as an instrument of conversion. It provided concrete visions of "womanly" existence like mine, yet not so like as to arouse my resistance to disparagement. This was, after all, the only life I'd known, and I had a lot invested in it; calling it into question directly was simply too risky. Through literature I could call some *other* woman's life into question, identify with its terms gradually, and discover in my own good time that I could write another life for myself.

I don't know now why I took so long to start this process (if indeed I *did* take long) or what I expected the outcome to be. I do know that whereas Woolf's obsessions, at the first, struck too unsettlingly close to home, Doris Lessing's *Memoirs of a Survivor*, with its futuristic setting in a disintegrating city, proved just remote enough so that I could, in the course of analyzing "a woman's" life, begin to discern the contours of my own. I also know that I'd already read

The Memoirs of a Survivor, as well as *The Four-Gated City*, five years earlier, and *The Golden Notebook* nearly a decade before that. Why hadn't any of them catalyzed the sort of critical revision I was now undertaking? What combination of life and literature prepares us for the leaps we make at one moment and not another? Had reading those books without apparent effect then made me ready to profit from one of them now? And why *this* one?

The Memoirs of a Survivor is an odd novel — "an attempt at autobiography" Lessing has called it. It unfolds — the word seems peculiarly apt for the multiple levels of experience it encompasses — as reminiscences within an anonymous female consciousness, that of the "survivor," who acts as observer and recorder of the incremental but wholesale breakdown of society and thus, symbolically, of the social hold on individual consciousness. The survivor's existence is fragmented between "ordinary" life and a series of visions perceived through her livingroom wall. Into her "ordinary" life wanders Emily, who matures within the brief span of the novel from a "half-grown girl" to a woman of thirty-five or forty, which is perhaps the survivor's age (and was also mine at the time the novel became useful to me).

As she ages in this foreshortened fashion, Emily becomes universalized, passing through clearly recognizable stages in white Western female development which excite in narrator and reader alike the shock of familiarity: "for my part, she, her condition, was as close to me as my own memories."[3] Emily begins as a bright child, painfully anxious to please; as she enters adolescence, becoming dreamy and self-absorbed, she eats constantly. Discovering boys, she stops eating and fabricates out of old clothes a series of fantastic self-portraits, until, "chyrsalis after chrysalis . . . out-grown,"[4] she emerges, conventionally clad, to join one of the gang of young people now continually roving the streets.

After a period of experimentation, she falls in love. Collecting a group of abandoned children, she and her beloved Gerald establish a "family," with Emily as unwilling but effective matriarch. She has an intense relationship, perhaps lesbian, with a younger woman; loses this woman, as well as her family and Gerald, in the increasing social chaos; becomes at last

> a mature woman, a woman who has had her fill of ev-erything, but is still being asked from, demanded of, persuaded into giving. . . . She loves—oh, yes, but somewhere in her is a deadly weariness. . . . She knows herself—the eyes of men and boys say so—as a source; if she is not this, then she is nothing. So she still thinks—she has not yet shed that delusion. She gives. She gives. But with this weariness held in check and concealed . . . she would never willingly suffer any of it again.[5]

Emily and the survivor are, in fact, projections of a single self: the survivor had been Emily, but to be Emily is to be, by definition, nonreflective; now she learns who she has been. And if "deadly weariness" were the culmination of her development, as I feared it to be in my own, then life would be unendurable. But the survivor finds herself "waiting for (just as somewhere inside herself [Emily] must be) . . . the moment she would step off this merry-go-round, this escalator carrying her from the dark into the dark. Step off entirely. . . . And then?"[6] It is possible, she glimpses, to step off the merry-go-round or the escalator—the one traveling in fixed circles, the other along fixed lines—to move in some other manner.

Reflecting Lessing's interest in Jungian psychoanalysis and in Sufism, the survivor's discovery of an alternative way of being comes not from "ordinary" life but from "behind the wall," from dreams. Some of these—the limiting, stifling dreams of the "personal"—offer her insights into what it means to become a woman, particularly in social terms, by depicting scenes from Emily's past. Other, archetypal dreams, which take place largely in a shifting set of rooms, hold the possibility of an integrated self united with Absolute Being, the "*exiled* inhabitant" of the rooms,[7] whom the survivor does not see until the very end. In these,

> very strong was the feeling that I did as I was bid and as I must; that I was being taken, was being led, was being shown, was held always in the hollow of a great hand which enclosed my life, and used me for purposes I was too much beetle or earthworm to understand.
>
> Because of this feeling, born of the experiences behind the wall, I was changing. A restlessness, a hunger that had been with me all my life, that had always been accompanied by a rage of protest (but against what?) was being assuaged. I found that I was more often simply waiting. I watched to see what would happen next. I observed. I looked at every new event quietly, to see if I could understand it.[8]

Very gradually, the world of "ordinary" life and the one "behind the wall" converge until the barrier between them dissolves and the survivor attains her final vision: the self emerges whole, free from the fragments of both ordinary life and the dream world, leading all the parts of her existence—Emily and Gerald and even the beastly children, all accepted and intergrated—"out of this collapsed little world into another order of world altogether."[9] From that world she writes back—words of encouragement, as it were. For she is not alone there. In her first sentence, "We all remember that time," she lets us know that others with her have lived through and then broken free from biologically and culturally determined experiences, have with patience and courage pulled together the elements of personality fragmented by past pressures and present expectations, have won for their efforts oneness. Through their shared experience they form a community: "this is what, looking back, we acknowledge first—our similarities, not our differences."[10] And their progress holds a promise of spiritual regeneration and survival for everyone.

Even me. The figure of the survivor—no, more precisely, her rhetorical function—revealed the possibility that one could both construct and deconstruct one's life simultaneously, and that in so doing one might achieve an equilibrium I had strained for all my life, growing quiet, patient, alert, and curious. By scrutinizing my life I could see how it had been made and could also, if I wished (and oh, I wished!), change it. I could, if I chose, explore the mysteries without madness, without death. I could survive. All this could be done, *The Memoirs of a Survivor* made me see, but it did not let me know how I would go about the task outside the privileged confines of a fantasy novel. For that, I needed to return to Virginia Woolf, who has always for me best portrayed (no matter what the subject at hand) the conditions and limits of the writing life, which was the one I was determined to lead.

Especially in her later works, not unlike Lessing's survivor but with a broader vision, Woolf struggles to transcend a destructive past which binds and suffocates the present, foreseeing a future that is uncertain, potentially dangerous, but necessary for survival. The process is painful, and as a result Woolf's tone is sometimes elegaic, often melancholy. As she writes,

> If one is to deal with people on a large scale & say what one thinks, how can one avoid melancholy? I don't admit to being hopeless though—only the spectacle is a profoundly strange one; & as the current answers don't do, one has to grope for a new one; & the process of discarding the old, when one is by no means certain what to put in their place, is a sad one.[11]

In work after work, both didactic and imaginative, she sketches the "current answers," discards them, and strives to determine "what to put in their place," her fundamental question the one that the elderly Eleanor asks at the end of one of Woolf's late novels, *The Years*: "And now? . . . And now?"[12] The struggle is thrilling, though the thrill is of fear as well as of hope.

I was, at best, an embryonic feminist when I began to steep myself in Woolf's writing, and now I'm grateful that I chanced to gestate there, for Woolf is appreciably more radical than many of the more recent writers available to me then. That is, she calls for culture to be altered at its root,

63

wholly transfigured, not merely modified to correct some perceived inequities between female people and male people.

Although I would have believed (and of course still do) that women and men should enjoy equal access to compensation for professional activities, for example, I would not yet have questioned whether professional life was wholesome for human beings of either gender, as Woolf does in *Three Guineas*:

> It is obvious that if you are going to make the same incomes from the same professions that those men make you will have to accept the same conditions that they accept. . . . You will have to leave the house at nine and come back to it at six. That leaves very little time for fathers to know their children. You will have to do this daily from the age of twenty-one or so to the age of about sixty-five. That leaves very little time for friendship, travel or art. You will have to perform some duties that are very arduous, others that are very barbarous. You will have to wear certain uniforms and profess certain loyalties. . . . In short, you will have to lead the same lives and profess the same loyalties that professional men have professed for many centuries.[13]

Nor, despite my activities in the peace movement during the Vietnam War, would I yet have consciously connected these lives and loyalties, as Woolf does, to the making of war.

At the end of *Three Guineas*, Woolf calls for the formation of an Outsiders' Society, belonging to women, whose fundamental duty is "to maintain an attitude of complete indifference" toward the fighting of men. Instead, outsiders are to earn their own livings and to eschew all public attention and honors, because "ease and freedom, the power to change and the power to grow, can only be preserved by obscurity; . . . if we wish to help the human mind to create, and to prevent it from scoring the same rut repeatedly, we must do what we can to shroud it in darkness." Woolf recognizes that she and the man to whom she addresses her essay are striving for the same end: "one world, one life." Nevertheless, she concludes, "we can best help you to prevent war not by repeating your words and following your methods but by finding new words and creating new methods."[14]

I had always believed myself to be an outsider, unlike others and unable to fit myself to their desires and demands, but that was just adolescent paranoia—you know, the sort of suspicion you get at a party that wherever the real action is taking place is anywhere you're not? In fact, in most ways I was an insider, a "daughter of educated men," as Woolf would put it. I'd always had enough to eat and plenty of clean clothes to wear, piles of books to read and instruction in reading them, respectable jobs, all the tickets to theatres and museums and concerts I could use. No one had ever told me to sit at the back of the bus. Except in antiwar demonstrations, I'd never been spat on. For me, as for Woolf, slipping "outside" presented something of a challenge. But choosing to move out there, I began to see, had a more than personal salvific force. Anyone who learned of the possibility was obliged to try. Maybe I could write my way out, finding "new words," "new methods."

In *Three Guineas*, Woolf's vision remains largely negative, a rejection of the traditional, male-dominated worldview as coercive, materialistic, destructive of men and women alike. Her approach here is analytical, and, as she notes in her diary, "ideas are sticky things; won't coalesce; hold up the creative, subconscious faculty."[15] Her creative powers, those enabling her to symbolize the issues and synthesize them into new patterns, flare up in the mystery and terror of *Between the Acts*, her last book. Completed but unrevised at the time of her suicide in 1941, this is, as Woolf herself called it, "more quintessential than the others. More milk skimmed off. A richer pat,"[16] the "poet's book" she had been promising herself for years. It has a simple surface. The action, which entails the staging of a village pageant depicting (sometimes hilariously) the whole of English history, occurs at an English manor house, Pointz Hall, within a time period of only about twenty-four hours, and involves few central characters. But the tangled question at its core, though unvoiced, is the same that motivates *Three Guineas*: How are we to prevent war? Its condemnation of the old, male-dominated order is even more uncompromising, and the need for a new vision more urgent and problematic.

In *Between the Acts*, the task of finding "new words" falls explicitly to the writer and director of the pageant, the outsider Miss La Trobe—withdrawn, lesbian, of unknown origins, with a foreign-sounding name that makes her presumably not "pure" English, features that suggest Russian blood, and a manner that makes her seem not "altogether a lady."[17] She must envision the answer to the novel's central question, which is nothing less than humanity's survival, and communicate it to her audience, thereby transforming them; failing, she must start afresh. That's what creators do, over and over: they fail and start afresh.

Like Woolf herself, Miss La Trobe attempts first to preserve and purify the old order by presenting a fresh perspective on it, in the hope that she will excite in her audience a sense of common purpose. And for a moment at the end of the pageant, her vision prevails, until it is shattered by "twelve aeroplanes in perfect formation,"[18] making clear that life as we have known it, our cultural heritage, civilization as a whole, despite its obvious and often poignant beauties, is too corrupt to be rescued. Looking at it from unconventional angles may provide new insights, but these are fleeting, fragmentary; they dissipate, leaving the isolation and the old antagonisms that have always threatened to destroy us. The pageant ends. The audience is dispersed. And Miss La Trobe betakes herself, alone, to the nearest pub, which is precisely what any sensible thwarted writer would do.

Her failure to effect more than a fleeting transformation necessitates a far more radical solution, not a fresh perspective on the old order but the creation of an entirely new one. First come chaos and dissolution into the primal elements, however, a movement that occurs, at the end of *Between the Acts*, both in the mind of Miss La Trobe and in the relationship between Isa and Giles Oliver, the owners of Pointz Hall. Before her creative vision begins, Miss La Trobe experiences the return of the earth to its primal state: "It was strange that the earth, with all those flowers incandescent—the lilies, the roses, and clumps of white flowers and bushes burning green—should still be hard. From the earth green waters seemed to rise over her. She took her voyage away from shore." She then sinks, symbolically, into the primordial ooze: "She raised her glass to her lips. And drank. And listened. Words of one syllable sank down into the mud. She drowsed; she nodded. The mud became fertile. Words rose above the intolerably laden dumb oxen plodding through the mud. Words without meaning—wonderful words." From this inchoate matter springs the new vision: "There was the high ground at midnight; there the rock; and two scarcely perceptible figures. Suddenly the tree was pelted with starlings. She set down her glass. She heard the first words."[19]

In silence, after the old people who are tied to the past and present have gone to bed, Giles and Isa move into the primeval world Miss La Trobe has conceived:

> The great hooded chairs had become enormous. And Giles too. And Isa too against the window. The window was all sky without colour. The house had lost its shelter. It was night before roads were made, or houses. It was the night that dwellers in caves had watched from some high place among rocks. . . . Alone, enmity was bared; also love. Before they slept, they must fight; after they fought, they would embrace. From that embrace another life might be born. But first they must fight, as the dog fox fights with the vixen, in the heart of darkness, in the fields of night.[20]

It is an awful vision, fraught with danger, providing no assurance that the new order will be any better than the old. Yet it offers some hope of "another life"—not just a child to carry on the traditions of the race but an other life, a different race, an alternative basis for the relationships between the dwellers in caves.

The scene between Isa and Giles composes itself in terms

of Miss La Trobe's vision, as though, in fact, life takes its form from art. The role of the artist is to speak the words out of which arise new heaven and new earth. The problem is, of course, that language is essentially a conservative as well as a creative force. We can talk about the future only in terms that also signify and fix the past and the present. A complete break with the masculine elements that encode the past and present requires that we not "talk about" the future at all. The attainment of the new order therefore requires a stupendous leap of faith, for Woolf's vision ultimately rests in a realm beyond language. Lessing's survivor has encountered precisely the same difficulty in stepping from one world into another: "All I can say is . . . nothing at all."[21]

And yet neither Lessing nor Woolf says nothing at all. Writers don't. Writers throw themselves forward into the unspeakable future on ropes of utterance and send back words, and if you're lucky, as I have been with Woolf and Lessing, you'll hear them as words of encouragement.

In the short term, the transformative visions of these writers did me no discernible good. I went mad anyway, in spite of or even because of them, and very nearly committed suicide. Old habits die hard. For about thirty years, I'd been muttering and moaning: *I want to write so much I could just die*. If I kept merely *wanting* to write, it appeared pretty likely that I would die. Instead, I reached for a pen.

I don't mean I took up writing as therapy. Although I don't doubt that writing can have remedial value, I've never been much interested in this aspect of it, maybe because I associate it with my months in a mental hospital, when an occupational therapist labored doggedly to get me to sit in a stuffy little room with some other patients and weave potholders. I didn't want to mend my life. I didn't want to restore my life to its old order. I'd gone through my chaos and dissolution. As I began to grow increasingly calm and watchful, I aimed to experience, with Virginia Woolf, "the strangest feeling now of our all being in the midst of some vast operation; of the splendour of this undertaking—life; of being capable of dying: an immensity surrounds me."[22] I was ready to write another life: out here, on the edge, in the wild.

I have. I go on.

Essaying the Feminine: From Montaigne to Kristeva

*t*he symbolic categories *masculine* and *feminine* usually align themselves with biological and social distinctions between *male* and *female, man* and *woman*, but they needn't always, as is clear in our ability to speak of a masculine woman or a feminine man without raising any questions about chromosomes or genitalia. Masculinity and femininity may in fact be organized around various loci of distinction.

Virginia Woolf, for instance, makes them a matter of dominance and submission in both the public and private spheres. Woolf identifies the masculine with "the creature, Dictator as we call him when he is Italian or German," Father we call him at home, "who believes that he has the right, whether given by God, Nature, sex or race is immaterial, to dictate to other human beings where they shall live, what they shall do," a stance that must be countered by a feminine "attitude of complete indifference" to the pomp and circumstance, the costumes, the patriotic sentiments that characterize the "manly qualities" leading to war.[1]

Julia Kristeva formulates the distinction in terms of time: "Female subjectivity would seem to provide a specific measure that essentially retains *repetition* and *eternity* from among the multiple modalities of time known through the history of civilization," in contrast to "a certain conception of time as project, teleology, linear and prospective unfolding; time as departure, progression, and arrival—in other words, the time of history."[2]

It is still possible in these structures to associate *masculine* with the male human being and *feminine* with the female. But Kristeva herself warns,

> The fact that these two types of temporality (cyclical and monumental) are traditionally linked to female subjectivity insofar as the latter is thought of as necessarily maternal should not make us forget that this repetition and this eternity are found to be the fundamental, if not the sole, conceptions of time in numerous civilizations and experiences, particularly mystical ones. The fact that certain currents of modern feminism recognize themselves here does not render them fundamentally incompatible with "masculine" values.[3]

Many French theorists, Kristeva among them, carry the terms *masculine* and *feminine* to a level of abstraction at which they become principles or modalities without specific human referents. Thus, Kristeva postulates a female principle repressed, denied, and exiled by the Masculine Logos.[4] In other words, "the feminine," as everything left out by language, can't be articulated by either men or women. Such theorists have been criticized on the grounds that in accepting "the premise that language and experiences are coextensive," postulating "language to be a male construct whose operation depends on women's silence and absence," and "perceiving the project of representation [of women] as invalid," they "may settle for a textual 'femininity' unconnected to real women."[5]

The concept of textual femininity—of all that can never be said lying between and beneath the words on the page—unattached to some human form whose breasts and belly, swollen like the Venus of Willendorf's, insist upon its femaleness, has appeal (and not just for those men who use it to calm their queasiness about the exclusions women complain of: "But you see, dear lady, my femininity is just as repressed as yours"). It accurately, if paradoxically, reflects the female sense of functioning as a cipher in a symbolic system that does not represent her at all, her sense, that is, of not being a real *anything*, woman or otherwise, but only "the blank in the symbolic chain, its hole."[6]

And yet—historically, culturally, existentially—there have been real women (as there have been real men): not just modalities but cellular constructs, warm and wet and fragrant and surprisingly durable, occupying some space, some time, who have (whether reasonably or not) believed themselves not men and have therefore experienced some difference whereby they have been known to represent themselves as women. I can't prove this statement, of course. I only know it in my bones. The nature of their womanness may well be influenced by their function as silences in male-dominated language: their negativity, their dissidence, as Kristeva would have it.[7] But it is *theirs*, it attaches to them as female human beings as it does not to male human beings, because they bear the weight of centuries of living according to certain terms, under a certain law, as it were, which has marked them experientially as a separate caste. Thus, the feminine is more than a symbolic category.

74

In my writing, I try to sustain a kind of intellectual double vision: to see the feminine *both* as that which language represses and renders unrepresentable by any human being, male or female, *and* as that which in social, political, and economic terms represents experiences peculiar to the female. I want my femininity both ways—indeed, I want it as many ways as I can get it. I am the woman writer. Don't ask me for impregnable argument. As far as I'm concerned, my text is flawed not when it is ambiguous or even contradictory, but only when it leaves you no room for stories of your own. I keep my tale as wide open as I can. It's more fun this way. Trust me.

Like the French feminists, I subscribe to the premise that the world we experience is itself an immense text that in spite of its apparent complexity has been made in Western thought to rest on a too-simple structural principle opposing reason to emotion, activity to passivity, and so on, every pair reflecting the most basic dichotomy—"male" and "female." Like them, I seek to disrupt the binary structure of this text, or Logos, through *l'écriture féminine*, which "not only combines theory with a subjectivism that confounds the protocols of scholarly discourse, it also strives to break the phallologic boundaries between critical analysis, essay, fiction, and poetry."[8]

Hence I write essays in the Montaignesque sense of the word: not the oxymoronic "argumentative essays" beloved by teachers of composition, which formalize and ritualize intellectual combat with the objective of demolishing the opposition, but *tests*, trials, tentative rather than contentious, opposed to nothing, conciliatory, reconciliatory, seeking a mutuality with the reader which will not sway her to a point of view but will incorporate her into their process, their informing movement associative and suggestive, not analytic and declarative.

"If my mind could gain a firm footing," writes Montaigne, "I would not make essays, I would make decisions; but it is always in apprenticeship and on trial."[9] In fact, the details of Montaigne's life demonstrate that he was fully capable of making decisions; in his essays he sets aside that capacity. "Thus his starting points are not intended to engage a war of opinions," says John O'Neill of the Montaignesque writer, "they are rather subjunctive alliances for the sake of exploring what hitherto had been shared terrain. By the same token, the conclusions reached are not meant to be absolute, but only what seems reasonable as a shared experience." And, as O'Neill points out, "Montaigne found thinking difficult because he rejected the easy assembly of philosophy and theology careless of man's embodied state," aware that the "loss in scholastic abstractions is that they can be mastered without thought and that men can then build up fantastic constructions through which they separate the mind from the body, masters from slaves, life from death, while in reality nothing matches these distinctions."[10]

Preference for relation over opposition, plurality over

dichotomy, embodiment over cerebration: Montaigne's begins to sound like a feminist project. Which is not to say that Montaigne was a feminist. ("You are too noble-spirited," he was able to write to the Comtesse de Gurson when she was expecting her first child, "to begin otherwise than with a male.")[11] But whether intentionally or not, Montaigne invented, or perhaps renewed, a mode open and flexible enough to enable the feminine inscription of human experience as no other does. The importance of this contribution has been largely overlooked, perhaps because many of Montaigne's statements, as well as his constant reliance on prior patriarchal authority, strike one as thoroughly masculine, and also because the meaning of *essay* has traveled so far from Montaigne's that the word may be used to describe any short piece of nonfiction, no matter how rigid and combative.

"Thus, reader, I am myself the matter of my book," Montaigne writes in his preface to the essays. "You would be unreasonable to spend your leisure on so frivolous and vain a subject."[12] In claiming this plural subjectivity, he is clearly aware that he has made writing do something new: "Authors communicate with people by some special extrinsic mark; I am the first to do so by my entire being, as Michel de Montaigne, not as a grammarian or a poet or a jurist."[13] Not much later, Francis Bacon, the first English writer of "essays," would shape modern scientific method thus: "Generally let every student of nature take this as a rule—that whatever his mind seizes and dwells upon is to be held in suspicion, and that so much the more care is to be taken in dealing with such questions to keep the understanding even and clear."[14] How differently Montaigne perceives the human psyche in essays that are, as Virginia Woolf notes, "an attempt to communicate a soul . . . to go down boldly and bring to light those hidden thoughts which are the most diseased; to conceal nothing; to pretend nothing; if we are ignorant to say so; if we love our friends to let them know it."[15]

This image of descent and retrieval echoes Woolf's description elsewhere of the experience of the woman writer as a dreaming fisherman whose imagination sweeps "unchecked round every rock and cranny of the world that lies submerged in the depths of our unconscious being," seeking "the pools, the depths, the dark places where the largest fish slumber," until it smashes against the rock of "something, something about the body, about the passions, which it was unfitting for her as a woman to know." This problem, "telling the truth about my own experiences as a body, I do not think I solved," says Woolf.[16] In such an adventure, Montaigne has the advantage, his embodiment and his awareness of it owning at least marginal cultural acceptability. Even so, his task is hardly easy, Woolf writes, for he must be "capable of using the essayist's most proper but most dangerous and delicate tool," the self: "that self which, while it is essential to literature, is also its most dangerous antagonist."[17]

It is this quality in Montaigne that Woolf admires, and often imitates in her own essays, despite her self-doubt: "this talking of oneself, following one's own vagaries, giving the whole map, weight, colour, and circumference of the soul in its confusion, its variety, its imperfection."[18] Not command of the mind and the world, but communication with the mind and its world forms Montaigne's purpose. "I do not portray being: I portray passing," he states, characterizing his project as "a record of various and changeable occurrences, and of irresolute and, when it so befalls, contradictory ideas: whether I am different myself, or whether I take hold of my subjects in different circumstances and aspects."[19] By embracing contradiction, Montaigne never permits himself a stance sturdy enough for gaining sovreignty over himself, his fellow creatures, or any of the other natural phenomena objectified by scientific discourse.

Unlike Montaigne, Bacon had no qualms about his footing. All a man need do was dislodge the idols of his mind—rooted in human nature, idiosyncracy, social intercourse, and philosophical dogma—and he would see plain the objective world, the world "out there," the world of principles uncontaminated by human flux and context. Human nature being pretty much as Bacon thought it was, "prone to suppose the existence of more order and regularity in the world than it finds,"[20] Bacon's detached view prevailed over Montaigne's messy, shifting, "domestic and private" engagement with "a life subject to all human accidents." For the past four hundred years, people may have read Montaigne for delight, even for wisdom, but most have turned to Bacon for direction to "the truth." And now, from the very products of Baconian practice, those trained in "scientific objectivity," we are learning that one cannot observe reality without changing it and that even physics, that quintessential exercise in intellectual aloofness, is not actually the impartial scrutiny of phenomena "out there" but is rather "the study of the structure of consciousness."[21]

In rejecting the concept of himself as a self-consistent

entity, purged of peculiarity, coherent through time and separate from the external processes he observes and records, Montaigne seems curiously contemporary, capable of grasping as Bacon would probably not what Michael Sprinker describes as "a pervasive and unsettling feature in modern culture, the gradual metamorphosis of an individual with a distinct, personal identity into a sign, a cipher, an image no longer clearly and positively identifiable as 'this one person.' "[22] "We are all patchwork," Montaigne writes, "and so shapeless and diverse in composition that each bit, each moment, plays its own game. And there is as much difference between us and ourselves as between us and others."[23] His use of the essay form reflects this sense of fragmentation.

Montaigne's essays are not strictly autobiographical if we accept the conventional definition of autobiography, the story of a person's life written by himself, wherein "story" is a narrative, that which has a beginning, middle, and (problematic) end: linear, continuous, coherent, chronological, causal. But insofar as the "life" in autobiography—selflifewriting—is a construct of the writing/written self, it has at least submerged narrative elements that may be read even when they are not explicit in the autobiographical text.[24] With its " 'stuttering,' fragmented narrative appearance,"[25] Montaigne's form helps him to avoid "the original sin of autobiography," the use of hindsight to render his narrative logically consistent,[26] as well as to mitigate the "split intentionality" between Montaigne the man and the discursive "I."[27] A collection of personal essays literally stutters—begins, halts, shifts, begins anew—in a partial and piecemeal literary enterprise that may go on, as Montaigne's did, for twenty years, ending or, more precisely, reaching "not their end but their suspension in full career"[28] only with death.

"To the extent that we impose some narrative form onto our lives," Phyllis Rose writes, "each of us in the ordinary process of living is a fitful novelist, and the biographer is a literary critic."[29] So, too, the autobiographer, whose interpretive task is complicated by a double authority and at least a triple subjectivity, since autobiography is the written (the root so demands) story (the word leaves room for the confabulative possibilities in the process) one tells oneself (first, always) and the wider world (some of whom, at least, are strangers), at some distance from the events and the responses of the subject (also oneself) to those events, about oneself. But the task may be more than complicated, it may be impossible, for the female autobiographer, who has been entitled—historically, culturally, linguistically, critically, that is, politically—to neither authority nor subjectivity. I distinguish the female autobiographer here because I believe her situation to be genuinely separable from that of any other selflifewriter. Margaret Homans articulates the type of difference I have in mind neatly in her discussion of the novels of Toni Morrison, Alice Walker, and Margaret Atwood:

> Indeed, among scholars who accept the primacy of language, one of the most vexed questions in feminist literary criticism is whether or not anything differentiates women's relation to discourse from other literary revolutions (modernism is the example most often cited), or from the discourse of other marginalized groups, such as colonial writers, or racial and ethnic minorities. . . . These novels differentiate between two kinds of margin-

ality: while victimization takes relatively overt forms with respect to race or nationality, the silencing and oppression experienced by women as women are masked as their choice.[30]

Thus, in the paradigm Elaine Showalter borrows from anthropologists Edwin and Shirley Ardner, because women, like minorities, occupy the "muted" cultural sphere, they must use the language of the "dominant" sphere if they expect to be broadly understood, because those who dominate will not trouble to learn their language.[31] Since the dominant language, organized on the basis of sexual polarity, controls the way we all look at the world,[32] and since "complicity with an oppressive male authority is a shared women's experience,"[33] a woman's capacity for uttering what is distinctive about her self's life is especially blunted. Her mutedness tends to become muteness.

Even leaving aside the crude but common identification of autobiography as a record of the great deeds of great men, one finds that until quite recently almost every discussion of the autobiographical project employs the generic "he." The hidden assumption that the self in selflifewriting is masculine is not, of course, surprising, but the absence of surprise does not signify the absence of pain. If we are all, in fact, fitful novelists, and the novel is a male genre; if the biographer and autobiographer are literary critics, and literary criticism is a male genre; then the female practitioner of *life*, let alone of selflifewriting, is inauthentic, forced to tell a story that is not hers. The act of telling, the act of writing about the telling, the very language of the telling and the writing exclude her experientially and aesthetically from her autonomous existence, make her function in the existence of an other, leave her at best skewed and strained, at worst silent as the grave.

How does the fitful novelist learn to inscribe his life/text? Here is the privileged process feminist criticism reveals: The writer, in imitating and recombining the inscriptions available to him from the context he calls culture, is literally the author of his being, with the authority to insert his own text forcefully into the world-text, which will validate the terms of his text, his way of being in the world. And once he lifts his pen to make of his inscription an artifact, his act joins the lineage of such acts, authorized by them, authorizing them, entering "the metaphor of literary paternity" wherein

82

> a literary text is not only speech quite literally embodied, but also power made manifest, made flesh. In patriarchal Western culture, therefore, the text's author is a father, a progenitor, a procreator, an aesthetic patriarch whose pen is an instrument of generative power like his penis. More, his pen's power, like his penis's power, is not just the ability to generate life but the power to create a posterity to which he lays claim.[34]

Ah yes, we've met this man before: He is the father of sons.

The female fitful novelist possesses no such paternal authority. Her attempts to tell herself the story of herself are cast in a syntax and lexicon demanding that she be the object, not the author, of desire—the stuff, not the spinner, of dreams. Not for her the pen/penis but only envy of the pen/penis. She lives as a lack. "A lot is being said today about the influence that the myths and images of women have on all of us who are products of culture," writes Adrienne Rich.

> I think it has been a peculiar confusion to the girl who tries to write because she is peculiarly susceptible to lan-

guage. She goes to poetry or fiction looking for *her* way
of being in the world, since she too has been putting
words and images together; she is looking for guides,
maps, possibilities; and over and over in the "words'
masculine pervasive force" of literature she comes up
against something that negates everything that she is
about: she meets the image of Woman in books written
by men.[35]

What she sees in the mirror of these texts may be beautiful
or hideous, but it is always unutterably alien. Yet if she tries to
articulate her self, these are the features that she limns: not
who she is but who she is for the man who desires / does not
desire her. Of her own desire she knows almost nothing. How
can she in a world-text whose language is predicated, according to the fathers of psychoanalysis and linguistics, upon lack
and rupture? In that context, the child learns to speak only to
name what is absent, irretrievably lost: the body of the mother,
riven from the child by the father, who introduces the wider
social world founded on sexual difference. According to
Jacques Lacan, without the phallus, then, the point of division,
the child does not enter language—the process of signifying
what is missing—and will not become an "I."[36] In this
account, woman is confined to the role of the Other—cipher,
secret, naught—who confers but does not derive meaning. In
the grammar of the phallus—the I, I, I—she can't utter
female experience.

"It is from the Other that the phallus seeks authority and
is refused,"[37] and refusal sounds like just what's called for
here. One alternative linguistic scheme might be based in
plenitude and continuity. Suppose we say that instead of loss of
the maternal body (which female children are "forbidden" less
radically than male children) as the means of entering the

symbolic order, the child luxuriates in the language spilling from that body freely and sweetly as milk until—so closely does she identify with the source of this pleasurable flow, so abundantly does she love the mother—she begins to reciprocate. And even after the two part, as the child's growing body and boundless curiosity dictate they must, they use words to signify their profound connection to each other and to all those (beginning with the father, phallus and all) who, over time, are drawn into their company. A writer, novelist Abby Frucht reflects, "doesn't look with her eyes, she looks with her words. She doesn't listen with her ears, she listens with her words. She doesn't touch with her fingers, she touches with her words."[38] Language may be imagined as a series of acts, both generous and generative, which do not mourn absence but affirm presence: word as glance, as sigh, as caress.

My concern here is not which of these linguistic views is correct—both are metaphors for a process still not fully understood—but which one permits all the figures caught up in it the richest development. The interpretive models we choose matter. The person who believes that in universal grammar the sentence "has a perpetrator and a victim, and often a blunt object, which is usually 'the,'"[39] does not occupy the same world as the one who supposes the sentence to hold two entities, who are often particularized by "the," in relation to each other. The woman who theorized language along the lines of intimacy might elude the text that phallogocentrism has coerced her into inscribing and tell some altogether different tale.

In 1929, Virginia Woolf caught glimpses of women writing "as women write, not as men write,"[40] but she predicted that it would be century before they realized their capabilities, and we've got more than a quarter of that span to go. Still, there are signs, there are visions of what woman's writing might look like. Here's one I particularly like, Hélène Cixous's description of "a feminine textual body" as

> always endless, without ending: there's no closure, it doesn't stop, and it's this that very often makes the feminine text difficult to read. For we've learned to read books that basically pose the word "end." But this one doesn't finish, a feminine text goes on and on and at a certain moment the volume comes to an end but the writing continues and for the reader this means being thrust into the void. These are texts that work on the beginning but not on the origin. The origin is a masculine myth. . . . The question, "Where do I come from?" is basically a masculine, much more than a feminine question. The quest for origins, illustrated by Oedipus, doesn't haunt a feminine unconscious. Rather it's the beginning, or beginnings, the manner of beginning, not promptly with the phallus in order to close with the phallus, but starting on all sides at once, that makes a feminine writing. A feminine text starts on all sides at once, starts twenty times, thirty times, over.[41]

Without specific examples, to which Cixous seems constitutionally averse, this definition is merely suggestive, however; and Woolf, though generally a marvel of precision, quotes a "man's sentence" readily enough but never sets down a comparable "woman's sentence." She does note some possible qualities of a woman's book—brevity, broken sentences and sequences—and of the sensibility producing it, most tellingly that "men were no longer to her 'the opposing faction' "[42] or perhaps even the objects of any particular interest at all.

The trick, as Woolf prescribes it, is somehow to "bring

out and fortify the differences" between masculine and feminine creative powers and enable a woman to write "as a woman" even though "it is fatal for any one who writes to think of their sex,"[43] and Woolf does not resolve this apparent dilemma. Can one *be* "woman," *do* "woman," but not *think* "woman?" And if one can't, will one truly expire? Well, probably not. A writer always writes out of difference, not just of gender but of every circumstance, and awareness of her idiosyncracies is likely to strengthen her work if only because it enhances her control of them. For a constellation of reasons, among them her own abuse in childhood,[44] sexual awareness may appear more problematic to Woolf then to many other writers. Such possible overreaction aside, however, her call for an androgynous mind undistorted by sex-consciousness may be construed as a matter not so much of attitude toward sex as of cognitive style. Woolf prefers the "union of man and woman" in the mind over their division into "opposing factions": a distinctively feminine (or possibly androgynous, but not masculine) view.

As my gropings here suggest, despite my instruction by a host of gifted feminist critics, I certainly don't yet have a clear vision of what women's writing might be. *Pace* Jacques Lacan, I know that the phallus is no transcendental signifier—nor transcendental anything else, as far as I'm concerned—but I don't know what my transcendental signifier is, if indeed there is any such thing, which I doubt, since the whole concept seems far too *located* to express my experience of the world. My "I" seems simply not to be the male-constructed "I.": It is more fluid, diffuse, multiplex (giddy, duplicitous, and inconstant, I think men have called it). Maybe we need another sort of signifier for the female

86

self—the "O" might be a logical choice, or rather a whole string of Os: OOOOO. That's me.

The fact of the matter, though, is that when I sit down at my desk to tell a story, I can't begin, "OOOOO woke this morning to the song of a cardinal in the fig tree outside the back door." Radical feminist writers like Monique Wittig and Mary Daly experiment with techniques for reinventing reality by exploding patriarchal linguistic patterns. But in passages like this one—

> The Powers to break the framers' frameworks are within women. Dis-Covering our Lust of Be-ing, we can easily swing open the doors to our freedom. We work to attain the Prudence of Prudes, the Courage of Crones, the Distemper of Dragon-identified Fire-breathing Furies. Furiously focused, we find our Final Cause.[45]

—all those hyphens and capital letters and puns and alliterations give me a wicked case of intellectual indigestion, and after twenty pages I'm too dyspeptic to go on. If I want to speak plainly to you about particulars—and I do, more than anything else—I must use the language that I know you know.

I want a prose that is allusive and translucent, that eases you into me and embraces you, not one that baffles you or bounces you around so that you can't even tell where I am. And so I have chosen to work, very, very carefully, with the language we share, faults and all, choosing each word for its capacity, its ambiguity, the space it provides for me to live my life within it, relating rather than opposing each word to the next, each sentence to the next, "starting on all sides at once . . . twenty times, thirty times, over": the stuttering adventure of the essay.

In Search of "In Search of Our Mothers' Gardens": Alice Walker

a few years back, in an attack of avarice, I got myself into a writerly pickle. The process of writing in order to pull together and plumb the ideas that my reading has yielded remains essential to my construction of the world. It's about the hardest work I know, however, and so left to my own devices I'm apt to work double-crostics or call around town getting estimates on upholstery cleaning instead. I live just a few blocks from the University of Arizona, and taking a course there now and then has encouraged me to undertake the kind of synthesis I'm talking about in a relatively painless manner. Actually, the first time I did this after I'd finish my Ph.D., taking a seminar in the personal essay with the late Edward Abbey, some pain turned out to be involved. For one thing, I had to read Hunter S. Thompson's *Fear and Loathing in Las Vegas*. For another, I was lonely—of a wholly different temperament from the other five students, and so much older than one sweet round blond pair that I could have been their mother (and the grandmother of the baby they produced in time for the last class). Worse yet, I was a feminist in a group whose awareness of women's issues extended only to the point of approving the fact that women could now be auto mechanics—and darned good ones, at that.

For a class presentation on a contemporary essayist, I decided that I wanted to do Alice Walker. I'd read only *The Color Purple*, but *The Color Purple* was quite enough to net me and hold me forever. And so, with the greedy enthusiasm that intoxicates me at the beginning of any course, I volunteered to do the first presentation so that I and no one else would get to do Alice Walker. I sobered up almost immediately, but by then my classmates had gone off to read *In Search of our Mothers' Gardens* in preparation for a presentation. Starting to read the book myself, I plunged almost instantly into despair. I had two weeks to prepare. I sensed before finishing the first essay that to do the right sort of job, I needed to read all of Alice Walker, as well as the work of Margaret Walker, Toni Morrison, Audre Lorde, Ann Allen Shockley, Toni Cade Bambara, Michele Wallace, and any number of other writers all the way back to Phillis Wheatley and especially Zora Neale Hurston, together with everything I could lay my hands on in black feminist theory. And even after this decade's work, I thought, I might fail to say anything meaningful about Alice Walker. For I was—

89

and am—intractably white and thus, possibly by my very nature, incapable of accurately reading a black writer.

My anxiety was rooted in the way I construe my responsibilities as a reader now that the New Critical purity of my undergraduate days is more than a quarter of a century behind me. Then, I believed in the effacement not just of myself but of the author as well in any critical act; who we are, Alice Walker and I, could have no effect on the immaculate text on the page. A number of influences have cracked the bell jar beneath which that vision was sealed, not the least of them being what literary theorist Nellie Furman calls "textual feminism," which recognizes "that we speak, read, and write from a gender-marked place within our social and cultural context."[1] And the place from which we read, speak, and write is race- and class-marked as well. Contemplating the task I'd taken on, I thought of Alice Walker, born a year after me, the eighth and last child of Georgia sharecroppers, and of me, the first child of a naval officer who died before I was five and a young college graduate who raised my sister and me in small New England towns. Might we not just as well have come from separate galaxies?

Because I am almost completely the product of a conventional literary education, I always risk standing in that intellectual space delineated by critic Barbara Smith: "Black women's existence, experience, and culture and the brutally complex systems of oppression which shape these are in the 'real world' of white and/or male consciousness beneath consideration, invisible, unknown."[2] "Beneath consideration" accuses me unfairly, since my temperament ranks virtually nothing beneath my consideration, which probably explains, though it does not excuse, my radical distractability. Issues of race and class loom larger in my consciousness as I mature, as they do in others' as well, though to suppose that they do so in everyone's consciousness is itself a kind of classist assumption common to "liberal" academics: anybody who *is* anybody takes race, class, and gender into account in her thinking about the world. A good many good people do not; and since condemning or dismissing them as racist/classist/sexist pigs suggests the very smugness one has set out to correct, enlightening "white and/or male consciousness" entails the tricky task of affirming their goodness while persuading them to become better.

But with regard to my experience, Smith is on the mark. For much of my childhood, black women and men were in fact "invisible, unknown": none lived in my town; I never traveled; both my schoolbooks and the novels I gobbled focused almost exclusively on Euro-American culture; for years I didn't even have a television or go to the movies, not that I was missing any meaningful representations of black reality by this lack. And since almost all my subsequent contacts have been casual, black life remains largely obscure to me. How could I ever speak of the woman who speaks of it?

In the end, Alice Walker herself forced me beyond my readerly timidity. Excoriating critic Patricia Meyer Spacks for failing to include black writers in her literary study *The Female Imagination* on the grounds that their experiences were unfamiliar to her, Walker writes, "Perhaps, however, this *is* the white female imagination, one that is 'reluctant *and unable* to construct theories about experiences I haven't had.'"[3] I was damned if I was going to let her call my imagination hesitant or helpless. It's a good imagination, a little kinky, maybe, but certainly no coward. What gave it this fit of faintheartedness was a lifetime of academic training, teacher after teacher admonishing me to trust not myself or the text but them and the authorities they'd direct me to. But they never taught me how to read a black woman. Just as well. Then and in the years since, I have let Alice Walker teach me to read Alice Walker.

I still think a decade's solid work would stand me in good stead, though I have read more African-American writing in recent years. But I still find the title essay in *In Search of Our Mothers' Gardens* admirably suited to the task of helping the inexperienced white reader reflect with clarity and confidence on "the black woman's philosophical problem," which is not wholly unrelated to her own, as stated by Nancy Hoffman: "How do I invent an identity for myself in a society which prefers to behave as though I do not exist?"[4] Unlike black male writers, who have tended to form part of that society even as another part has preferred to ignore their existence, Alice Walker faces a two kinds of marginality, and in the words of Margaret Homans, "while victimization takes relatively overt forms with respect to race or nationality, the silencing and oppression experienced by women as women are masked as their own choice."[5] As a result, the one may be confronted directly by language, but the other may have no ready form of expression. In order to utter the experience of black women, Walker must invent strategies, both structural and symbolic, which disrupt the pattern of expectations imposed by the dominant literary tradition—one of which is that black women have nothing to speak of—so that what has not been permitted to exist can come into being. "In Search of Our Mothers' Gardens" demonstrates some of these strategies.

In this essay, as in many of her other writings, Walker remakes the definitions of Art and the Artist (the very ones I'd first gone to graduate school to learn to do/become), which have resided from time immemorial in the patriarchal domain, so that they describe the African-American woman. To do so, she must so subvert the conventional meanings that they no longer have the power to exclude her. In the process, she employs and thereby validates many of the cognitive modes—indirection, associative reasoning, anecdotal development, reliance on folk wisdom and intuition—which patriarchal critics have traditionally devalued by ascribing them to women and other primitive thinkers.

The essay is a structural anomaly. I would hate to teach it in a traditional freshman composition course. After reading their textbooks, my students would go nuts trying to find the thesis statement and the major points of support for a formal outline, much less figure out its method of development and analyze its logical devices. (Interestingly, in the rhetorical index to *The Contemporary Essay*, where "In Search of Our Mothers' Gardens" is reprinted, it is listed only under "narration"—not even "description" or "example"—despite, or perhaps because of, the complexity of its rhetorical strategies.) In this day of nearly universal education, with handbooks for writers proliferating as fast as publishers can yank them (unproofread) off the presses, the five-paragraph essay has achieved the status of a cultural paradigm, which Walker blows to smithereens. Her essay has a structure, of course, one whose design is plain but idiosyncratic. It falls roughly into halves—the first, generally historical in focus, defining the black woman artist; the second, focused on personal history, defining the artist's work and ways; the two halves developed largely through example and linked by a pivotal central paragraph.

The twelve pages of the essay contain fifty paragraphs, a dozen of which consist of single sentences. The effect is staccato, emphatic: a quickened pace that conveys urgency. Syntactically, nine of her statements lack prediction. Nine sentences take the form of questions, some of which are answered immediately, others left to resonate in the reader's inner ear. Many contain interruptive dashes: "During the 'working' day, she labored beside—not behind—my father in the fields."[6] Many concatenate phrases with colons, sometimes in unorthodox ways: "And so our mothers and grandmothers have, more often than not anonymously, handed on the creative spark, the seed of the flower they themselves never hoped to see: or like a sealed letter they could not plainly read." Many, too, speak in the measured periods made familiar by Martin Luther King, Jr.: "They lay vacant and fallow as autumn fields, with harvest time never in sight: and he saw them enter loveless marriages, without joy; and become prostitutes, without resistance; and become mothers of children, without fulfillment." One group takes the form of a poem. Everywhere, as in poetry, the language is fluid, sometimes quirky, playing against convention to keep the reader unfixed, unlulled, open to Walker's search.

In addition to her own poem, Walker quotes four other authors. Her selection is revelatory. She opens with—takes off from—Jean Toomer, whom she characterizes elsewhere as having "a very feminine sensibility (or, phrased another way, he is both feminine and masculine in his perceptions), unlike most black male writers,"[7] and whose highly unorthodox novel *Cane* treats black women with unusual sensitivity.[8] She also quotes a fragment from the eighteenth-century slave Phillis Wheatley and her own paraphrase of a poem by the African Okot p'Bitek.

More than once she quotes from Virginia Woolf's *A Room of One's Own*. At first glance, this choice might seem surprising, since even in Woolf's own day she was accused of elitism, of failing to speak to or for any class but her own. But *A Room of One's Own*, one of the earliest and most brilliant feminist theoretical texts, remains radical in its insistence that "a woman must have money and a room of her own if she is to write fiction."[9] Moreover, Walker does not merely reprint, she revises Woolf's words. In each statement, she inserts into the English woman's history the realities of the black woman's history, broadening Woolf's view to encompass experiences of which Woolf would never have been aware:

> For it needs little skill and psychology to be sure that a highly gifted girl who tried to use her gift for poetry would have been so thwarted and hindered by contrary instincts [add "chains, guns, the lash, the ownership of one's body by someone else, submission to an alien religion"], that she must have lost her health and sanity to a certainty.   (Walker's interpolation)

In this way, Walker rescues Woolf's feminism for the black woman artist.

Following Woolf's pattern, Walker thinks back through the mothers who have enabled her art. Their creativity has taken many forms but, not surprisingly, except for the voice of Phillis Wheatley, crippled by contrary instincts, none rely upon the written word. Even those which are verbal—stories and songs—are not important primarily for their words. Of her mother's stories, "which came . . . as naturally as breathing" and which, in the fragmented life of a mother of eight children, were subject to "dying without conclusion," she says: "I have absorbed not only the stories themselves, but something of the manner in which she spoke, something of the urgency that involves the knowledge that her stories—like her life—must be recorded." Similarly, Phillis Wheatley's words do not much matter: "It is not so much what you sang, as that you kept alive, in so many of our ancestors, *the notion of song*." And it is not to the words but to the "voices of Bessie Smith, Billie Holiday, Nina Simone, Roberta Flack, and Aretha Franklin" that she commands us to listen. This is not Literature, not Music. This is storytelling, singing: the joy lies in the act, not in the artifact.

The other forms of creativity Walker ascribes to her foremothers have no words at all. Moreover, they, like the mother's broken-off story or the African woman's singing "*sweetly* over the compounds of her village," have no place in the canonical tradition of Art. They are women's work: the decorating of walls, the weaving of mats, the piecing and stitching of quilts, the planting of gardens. And because they stand outside the aesthetic tradition, at best marginalized as "crafts," they function as a language for the utterance of female experience, for which conventional discourse, shaped by the needs of male dominance, lacks the proper words. They articulate what feminist critic Elaine Showalter has called the "wild zone."[10]

The wild zone is the abode of female spirituality. Walker insists on talking about spirituality, a word that tends to cause the same sort of queasy lowering of eyes and quick conversational shifts that "bellybutton" might once have done. Of course you've got a spirit, darling—we all do—but we just don't talk about them in public. Alice Walker does. For her, the black woman artist *is* spirit. Spirituality is "the basis of Art," and if you suppress it, you drive the Creator to "a numb and bleeding madness." "I notice," she writes, "that it is only when my mother is working in her flowers that she is radiant, almost to the point of being invisible—except as Creator: hand and eye. She is involved in work her soul must have. Ordering the universe in the image of her personal conception of Beauty." In the expressing of art, even in a life, like her mother's, "so hindered and intruded upon in so many ways," the spirit becomes whole.

But the black woman artist is also a body, a body that brings forth daughters to whom she hands down "respect for the possibilities—and the will to grasp them." In "*One Child of One's Own*" she writes, "It occurred to me that perhaps white women feminists, no less than white women generally, cannot imagine black women have vaginas."[11] Once again, white imagination—my imagination—stands accused. Actually, although there was a long time when I had trouble imagining that *I* had a vagina, until I finally saw and believed, I have no trouble now imagining that women of any color have vaginas. And feeling certain of this imaginative capacity, I slough off the last scales of anxiety about my white middle-class incompetence to read Alice Walker. Outside the realm of patriarchal discourse, within its own interior, the body knows nothing of color or class.

97

Vaginas, Walker says. Admittedly, she needs to name a part of the body hidden from public scrutiny: *fingers* or *earlobes* would suggest an ignorance too far-fetched even for white women. But why not something less baldly anatomical—*heart*, say, or *womb*? In part because hearts and wombs already enjoy symbolic status in conventional discourse, both of them fraught with sentimentality. More importantly, however, hearts and wombs are sealed off from the external world, whereas vaginas connect inside to outside. They are avenues, not loci, and the traffic through them binds one being to another in complicated ways. The attachments they signify are carnal rather than sentimental.

This capacity for connection and continuity, shared by women of every color, constitutes a basis for artistic production and evaluation hitherto unacknowledged because unexperienced by the historical shapers of discourse. Walker, in uttering the unspeakable—*vagina*, not *heart* or *womb*—redeems lost territory. We came from vaginas, she reminds us; we have vaginas; out of our vaginas we have squeezed beings with vaginas, who may well do the same. And even if the topographical details of our wild zones aren't identical, the zones sure are thoroughly, wonderfully wild.

I think anew of my own mother, who has sewed me suits with hand-piped linings and hemmed my dresses with lace and knitted me heavy, intricate sweaters. And of my grandmother, whose recipes, written in her own hand, I treasure in my file, and who would not die until after she had poured the candied orange peel into the sterile jars to cool. And of my great-grandmother, whose language I never learned but whose crocheted coverlet lay in my cedar chest, safe from the claws of cats, until my daughter found a room of her own for it. And of all the spinners and weavers and Salem witches, lost to me and yet not lost: in me, speaking through me. I think, too, of my daughter, now embarked on a writing project, a teaching career, a marriage. And of the daughter I wish for her one day.

In search of *In Search of Our Mothers' Gardens*, and again each time I've returned to it, I have found bouquets and garlands of my own.

99

Reading Houses, Writing Lives: The French Connection[1]

*O*n a glittering August morning in 1979 at the edge of a salt marsh in Kennebunkport, Maine, I made a psychic sick.

I had never consulted a psychic before, though as a child I had wished I could accompany my mother and grandmother and take a turn having my cards read whenever they went over to Salem to a woman named Lal. Mother and Granna were two of the least spacey women I've ever known, smart and pragmatic and as ordinary in their beliefs and habits as two single matrons, one widowed and the other divorced, could be; and I can't imagine what lured them to Lal. But off they went to her, more than once in my recollection and perhaps before, returning deeply convinced of the accuracy of her predictive powers.

Whenever I asked to be taken to Lal with them, Mother and Granna told me I was too young. And then Lal stopped doing readings. She couldn't bear, they said, the accuracy of her insights when they involved disaster. So I never got my turn, and never gave my loss much thought. Then one day over lunch my friend Liz began to tell about a wonderful psychic she'd recently visited, and I felt my curiosity rekindle. "Why don't you give it a try?" my husband asked. (George never does anything weird himself, but he's very good at egging me on.) We were on vacation, without commitments, and the opportunity to take my children to Kennebunkport, where I'd spent part of my childhood summers, appealed to me. So I took the psychic's number and gave her a call that night to make an appointment.

On the scheduled morning we found the house easily, just across a little bridge on the main road into the village, and George dropped me off. He and the children would drive down to the beach and play for the hour or so I'd been told the reading would take. I felt a little nervous and shyer than usual.

The psychic, whose name I've long since forgotten, was very young and very pretty, with dark eyes and smooth, swingy dark hair set off by a delicate white summer dress. She led me through the house into a beautiful kitchen with an antique table and chairs at one end, overlooking through wide windows the silvery green marsh. We sat there, chatting a little awkwardly as I set up my tape recorder, which Liz had recommended I use so that I'd forget nothing. She took a deck of cards and began to lay them out, speaking in a light voice. I have no idea what she said, having lost the tape years ago.

Perhaps a minute or so passed before she put her hand to her forehead and complained of a headache. She tried to go back to the cards, then put her hand up again.

"There's something wrong with my eyes. My vision is so blurred I can hardly see the cards."

"I have multiple sclerosis," I told her as if to offer reassurance. "I have a scotoma, a blurry spot, in my right eye." She tried to attend to the cards again, without much luck.

"I just feel terrible," she said. "I don't know what's wrong. Maybe eating something would help." She took a reddened peach from a bowl on the sideboard behind her and bit it. She laid out a few more cards. "I'm not sure here," she said, squinting as if to focus. "I can't tell what these mean." She seemed reluctant to talk about the cards.

"Look, you don't have to go through this," I said. "I can leave."

"Oh, no," she protested without warmth.

"I'm going right now." I put the tape recorder in my bag and stood up.

"I'm so sorry," she said in a good-girl voice. "Perhaps I'm coming down with something. Listen, my in-laws live in Tucson and I'm going out to visit them this winter. Maybe I could do a reading for you then. Give me your name and address."

"Sure," I said, jotting them down. I'm not psychic, but I knew she'd rather die at this point than lay her blurred vision on me again. I made for the door.

I am a bit spacier than my mother and grandmother, but not much. Yet I felt so little doubt that my proximity was causing the psychic's distress that I was reluctant even to remain outside her house. I walked back up the road, across the bridge, and perched on the narrow railing there to pass the half-hour or so till George and the children returned for me. I sat in the startling sunshine, almost as bright as I was used to in the desert, and stared into the brown weedy water, pondering why the psychic had not been able to give me a coherent reading.

Kennebunkport had always been a powerful place for me, the most powerful in my world, in fact. My forebears had lived here, and my father lay in the small and slightly ragged cemetery a few miles up this road. Perhaps that was it. Or perhaps it was my physical condition, an incurable degenerative disease, lodging somehow in her sensitive flesh. Or perhaps she had seen something in the cards so terrible that she couldn't bear to read it to me, couldn't even bear to look at it herself. Though I didn't know it yet, I was already spiraling into a full-blown depressive episode, and by the same time a year later I would be almost lost. Now I look back and wonder if she sensed this danger. I wonder, too, whether if she had seen and warned me of it, I might have handled it better than I did.

As it was, I came away with only a fragmentary tape and a spookiness I couldn't quite communicate to George when he finally pulled up beside me and let me in. We drove on into the village, which I hardly recognized, so gentrified had it become with tourist dollars. We went up to my family's house, long since sold and converted into an apartment building. The veranda had been pulled off and the area

beneath it cemented to form a barren terrace. The cavern-
ous front hall, I saw as I peered through the glass in the
door, had been constricted by flimsy blond formica paneling
to a tiny square. Anne and Matthew, thirteen and ten that
summer, stared at the place vacantly, not even bothering to
puzzle out what magic their mother seemed to find in it.
They were a bit more intrigued by the cemetery and stood
respectfully enough at the foot of my father's grave. But they
have all their lives had a perfectly serviceable grandfather in
the person of my stepfather, and this one has no significance
for them even as a ghost.

Having stopped at the shrines, we drove back into the
village and walked around a little. It had all, even the Lyric
movie theater, been turned into little shops selling mostly
tasteful and pricey curios. The River View Restaurant was
still there, but remodeled and polished and so popular that
we couldn't get a table. We finally found a vacant little
restaurant on the other side of the river, where we got a late
lunch of fried clams before heading back down the coast.
That was the end of our trip to Kennebunkport. I would not
make another visit—happier, though just as brief—for
thirteen years.

What I didn't know that day, or for a good while
afterward, was that I'd begun to write a book. The psychic
never said. Something had shifted in me, like carelessly
stowed cargo, skewing my course almost imperceptibly at
the first, though later I'd fetch up here in an orange desk
chair in front of a word processor on a chilly November
afternoon, farther afield than I could have imagined then.
What moved me I'm not certain. In part, I was disturbed by
the psychic's refusal, whatever its cause, to "read" my life.

Something about that life now seemed, thanks to her denial, unreadable, alien, impermissible, as though I'd stepped outside for a minute and, the door blowing shut behind me, discovered that my key no longer fit the lock.

Then, too, there was the puzzle of the lost house, the lost town. *A* house was there, and *a* town, right were I had left them, but both they and I had been so transformed by the intervening years that they were, literally, not the ones I knew. The ones I knew were not there. But neither had they vanished altogether. They were perfectly present to me in both waking and sleeping dreams. They seemed to have sunk from their perch on the banks of the Mousam River into the brine of my own cells. I was the Port incarnate, all that was left of the place I meant by the Port, and the only return possible was involution.

Not long after that day on the coast of Maine, back in the desert soil I've chosen to nurture and chastise me, I bought a copybook and began to sketch some reminiscences of the houses I had grown up in as part of a preliminary study of women's autobiographical writing, but I didn't get far before other duties claimed me. Then, a year or so later, I returned to them in a workshop taught by a well-known southwestern writer of nonfiction. His response was glum: my memoirs were not readable, he wrote on the back of the last page, "to an ordinary bored, busy, hard-nosed, cynical, weary, cigar-smoking, whisky-drinking, fornicating old fart like—not me!—but your typical magazine or book editor. . . . Now if you were (already) a famous person this might not matter; but you're not; so it does." Well, I certainly wasn't a famous person. Not only that, but since I lacked the stature or stamina to take up football, and I was too old and funny-looking to pass a screen test, and I was more apt to hang out with the tramps at our local soup kitchen than with Beautiful People anywhere, I hadn't any chance of becoming a famous person. No fame, no life. I put the copybook with its blotchy black-and-white cardboard covers away.

I was, in some ways, a slow learner. At that time I didn't understand the kind of radical questioning that all moral life, but especially life in the academy, requires. I deferred to the values of the Fornicating Old Fart (FOF, let's call him for short) because he'd published a lot of books and I hadn't published any. In this way I remained open to his good advice—that I'd have to make my memoirs readable—but rendered it useless, since I had no permission now to write memoirs, readable or otherwise. What I didn't ask was first, whether FOF actually represented the audience I was writing for, and second, whether fame was an authentic qualification for a memoirist.

The answers to these questions unfolded for me slowly. I began to recognize that in fact nine-tenths of the literature I was familiar with had been written for FOFs—but it had also been written *by* FOFs, of which, by virtue of my gender, I could not be one. This literature forms what is known in conventional feminist parlance as the patriarchal literary canon, still firmly entrenched after centuries. So, if typical magazine or book editors were FOFs, I was going to have a tough time getting published no matter what. I could, of course, choose to write in the persona of an FOF; some women slipped by the gatekeepers of current literary taste that way. But I could also, thanks to the bravery and honesty of women writing before and beside me, choose not to. Some publishers employ editors like mine for *Remembering the Bone House* turned out to be: fresh, amused, energetic, supportive, open to quirky ideas, quick to praise. I don't think she ever smoked a cigar in her life.

As for a memoirist's fame, it's a requirement attached to the moldy definition of autobiography as the self-reporting of "the great deeds of great men." By this definition, no woman could ever compose a "life." Yet the earliest extant autobiography in English literature was dictated by a woman (illiterate, of course), fifteenth-century Margery Kempe; and similar claims have been made in other literatures. And women, whose access to fame has always been severely restricted, though notoriety has been more commodious, have continued to excel at autobiographical writing—memoirs, notebooks, letters, journals—to the present. Isak Dinesen wasn't famous when she penned *Out of Africa*, though, as it turned out, *Out of Africa* made her famous. She needed to make some money, her African coffee venture having turned financially disastrous, and she was desperately homesick for a land and a life permanently lost to her. The strength of that yearning, which sings on every page, has touched more readers than any "great" man's memories of his "great" conquest of the Dark Continent and its peoples.

The impulse to become famous, and to make a record of that famousness, arises out of the desire to distinguish oneself, to set oneself apart from (and preferably "above") the ordinary mass of humanity. As feminist psychologists like Nancy Chodorow have made clear, when mothers provide the primary care for all infants, as they do in our culture, this desire—for separation, for individuation—is more urgent from the outset in a boy. In order to establish his masculine gender identity, he must repudiate the person with whom he has identified initially and most powerfully. Girls, by contrast, whose gender identity will be the same as their mothers', "emerge with a stronger basis for experiencing another's needs and feelings as one's own . . . [and] come to experience themselves as less differentiated than boys, as more continuous with and related to the external object-world and as differently oriented to their inner object-world as well."[2]

If fame is predicated upon differentiation, and women experience differentiation in other ways than men do, then fame is likely to hold a distinctive value for them as well. I can't speak for other women. To be honest, I don't know how they feel about fame. The subject has never come up. Fame and its acquisition may be among those subjects banished from polite discourse. As for me, I recall a night when a friend prognosticated; "Nancy, one day you are going to be very rich and very famous." I laughed in reply: "Oh, I hope the 'rich' part comes true, but I don't know about fame. It seems like it would take up an awful lot of one's time." I supposed I might, like Virginia Woolf, find it "vulgar and a nuisance"[3] (and hoped, I'm sure, for the chance to find out). That's how it's always struck me, not as an evil to be avoided (some are corrupted by fame, to be sure, but others are not), but rather as a bothersome intrusion between oneself and the work one has chosen to do in the world. The work I have chosen demands connection, not separation: writing, weaving and mending relationships, serving people in need. Fame simply wouldn't be of use.

Thus, FOF and I have fundamentally disparate attitudes toward life (what one does day after day) and a "life" (the report one makes on the outcome of what one has done day after day). He demands that I so conduct my daily affairs as to attract public attention for my distinctions; then I will have something "worth" writing about, a "life" even an editor will look at twice, a "life," that is, which will sell. Now, I don't have any objections to selling books (remember, I liked the "rich" part), but neither have I found the prospect of selling them a motivation for writing them. What arouses me is the desire to contact others, to share my experiences with them, to stir them to recognition of the similarities that underlie their experiences and mine, to illuminate and delight in and laugh over the commonalities of human life. To this end, I *can't* be "a famous person," standing out from my audience, declaiming publicly my distinctions as a fabulously wealthy automobile company president, say, or a multiply reincarnated actress, or a venerable Speaker of the House of Representatives. I want my "life," in reporting the details of my own life, to recount, at the level beneath the details, the lives of others. No modesty is entailed here, simply the desire to celebrate the private rather than the public world of human habitation.

I took a long time to free myself of FOF's notion that one merits one's memoirs through acquiring fame, and to develop the divergent sense of purpose I'm describing. What returned me to my "life" wasn't a sense of this freedom and development, however. It was an accident of intellectual messiness. Because my thoughts are easily scattered, I try to read and assimilate one book at a time; but if another comes along to intrigue me, I'm apt to sneak a peek. Thus, while I was working my way through Gaston Bachelard's phenomenological study *The Poetics of Space*, a new translation I had ordered, *The Newly Born Woman*, by the French feminists Catherine Clément and Hélène Cixous, arrived in the mail, and I found myself shuttling back and forth between the books. Suddenly the two collided in my head, houses and female sexuality tumbling and tangling into the autobiographical project I wanted to do: a memoir of my life as a female body.

"Not only our memories, but the things we have forgotten are 'housed.' Our soul is an abode. And by remembering 'houses' and 'rooms,' we learn to 'abide' within ourselves,"[4] Bachelard writes. And "housing" for him is not an airy metaphor. He means by it the literal physical structures that have sheltered us all our lives, which "through dreams . . . copenetrate and retain the treasures of former days," so that "when memories of other places we have lived in come back to us, we travel to the land of Motionless Childhood, motionless in the way all Immemorial things are." For me, as for Bachelard, understanding the significance of habitations "is not a question of describing houses, or enumerating their picturesque features and analyzing for which reasons they are comfortable. On the contrary, we must go beyond the problems of description . . . in order to attain to the primary virtues, those that reveal an attachment that is native in some way to the primary function of inhabiting."[5] But for me the "roots of the function of inhabiting" are entwined inextricably with my gender, which shapes my relationships to both the spaces I occupy and the language in which I meditate on those spaces. Bachelard, by contrast, reveals no awareness of himself as a being engendered, in part, by the very structures, architectural and linguistic, that he contemplates.

A male French philosopher writing in the 1950s, Bachelard assumed a universality of experience that permitted him to write, without irony, "As a general thesis I believe that everything specifically human in man is *logos*."[6] To which contemporary French feminists might reply, "Ah, precisely!" For they have pointed out repeatedly the immemorial intimate connection between the phallus and the logos, both of which serve as emblems of power reserved for the masculine discursive subject.

In order to subvert such a connection, Cixous points out in her section of *The Newly Born Woman*, "now it has become rather urgent to question this solidarity between logocentrism and phallocentrism—bringing to light the fate dealt to woman, her burial—to threaten the stability of the masculine structure that passed itself off as eternal-natural, by conjuring up from femininity the reflections and hypotheses that are necessarily ruinous for the stronghold still in possession of authority."[7] At the root of the issue lies *authority*: the right of woman to author her own story, a right whose tenuousness is demonstrated in the sense of "author" as "one that fathers." Were woman to arrogate that authority to herself, "all the history," in Cixous's words, "all the stories would be there to retell differently."[8]

But the phallocentric nature of discourse makes any such project problematic because it is "the enemy," as Cixous says, "of everyone. Men's loss is different from but as serious as women's. And it is time to change. To invent the other history."[9] And what will be the burden of this new tale? Virginia Woolf knew more than half a century ago when, in

"Professions for Women," she confronted the difficulty of "telling the truth about my own experiences as a body," an act prohibited her by "the extreme conventionality of the other sex."[10] Centuries of cultural repression of the knowledge of woman-as-body mean, says Cixous, that "women have almost everything to write about femininity: about their sexuality, that is to say, about the infinite and mobile complexity of their becoming erotic." Almost everything still to write, but constrained by a discourse that proscribes the feminine erotic plot. A woman's only recourse is the "theft" of language with which to "write her body"—"the act that will 'realize' the un-censored relationship of woman to her sexuality."[11]

The body is a dwellingplace, as the Anglo-Saxons knew in naming it *banhus* (bonehouse) and *lichama* (bodyhome), and the homeliness of its nature is even livelier for a woman than for a man. Bachelard speaks of "inhabited space" as the "non-I that protects the I."[12] Woman may literally become that inhabited space, containing, in Cixous's words, "a thousand and one fiery hearths" of erotic desire and experiencing in childbirth "the not-me within me," thereby becoming the non-I that protects the I of the unborn child. Still, forced to function as man's Other and thus alienated from her self, "she has not been able to live in her 'own' house, her very body. . . . Women haven't had eyes for themselves. They haven't gone exploring in their house. Their sex still frightens them. Their bodies, which they haven't dared enjoy, have been colonized."[13] Through writing her body, a woman may reclaim the deed to her dwelling.

The reverberations of all these texts coalesced for me into

the project of exploring my own "felicitous space," to use Bachelard's phrase, the houses where I once lived and where, time collapsing through dreams, I continue to live today. In *Remembering the Bone House* I returned to them, reentered them, in order to discover the relationships they bear to my own erotic development and thus perhaps— because I'm ever aware of my self as a cultural, not merely a personal, construct—to feminine erotic development in general.

It is difficult to redeem "eroticism" from the limitations of "genitality." The sexual pleasure of those whose view of the world dominates our language arises from a specific point in space (and time as well, for that matter)—the penis, whose set of cultural meanings has been termed the phallus—and the world so represented is divided into binary categories (you got it/you don't). Since man's pleasure is localized in his penis, he assumes that woman's is confined to some opposite location. The logical choice is her vagina, since it so neatly goes in where he goes out. But it turns out that she doesn't, as Cixous puts it, "go round and round the supreme hole"[14] as he goes round and round the paramount pole. She is not simply opposite to but absolutely different from him. Her *jouissance* can't be confined to one place (and the vagina wasn't even, it turns out, a particularly good approximation).

The consequences of raising to consciousness the limitlessness of feminine *jouissance* are magnificent and terrible for women both as beings in the world and as writers. (They may be equally so for men, but that's men's business. "Don't speak for me," my husband always commands. So I'm not speaking.) As I have grown older and freer of the strictures of language, I have found charms in the smallest crevices of my embodied existence. My husband doesn't understand this, I know. He cannot imagine that I might, in good health, thrill to the sun-struck petunias on the white table on our back porch or the aromatic burst of fresh basil on my tongue as to his most passionate embrace. I can't explain it to him. I can't explain it to anyone. It's just the way I am.

114

For these reasons, "eroticism" has a more global meaning for me than language usually permits. This semantic dissonance caused me problems with friends who asked about *Remembering the Bone House* as I was writing. "An erotics of place and space," I would tell them, waiting for the wince, the furrow, the grin. The responses varied, but plainly they all assumed that I was writing "a dirty book." Well, maybe I was. In it I mention my body, certainly, quite a lot, even its secret places. Here and there I kiss, stroke, press, squeeze, even engage in sexual intercourse. Not as often, though, as I lie in bed, run across a playground, eat favorite foods, listen to the radio, tease my sister, roll in new snow. All these acts, happening to me as a body, shaping my awareness of my embodied self, form my erotic being. It is that process I seek in all my writing to capture and comprehend: how living itself takes on an erotic tone.

For a woman saturated to the bone in Calvinist tradition, such an exploration necessitates the healing of another Western patriarchal bifurcation: body/mind or body/spirit. I grew up in the belief that my intellectual/spiritual life, reflective of my "true" self, was separate from and superior to my life as a body. My body's appearance, which preoccupied me, was dismissed as beneath my concern. Its urges were denied, or at least deferred: I was "saving" myself for marriage. In adulthood, apparently, my bodily life might begin, and I suppose it did, at least in sexual terms. After I was married, I deliberately masturbated for the first time, so I must have believed myself entitled to my body's sensations in a new way. But I got through two pregnancies and childbirths, several sexual affairs, a couple of serious suicide attempts, and the onset of a devastating degenerative disease while locked almost entirely in my head.

115

My body, of course, was going through all these, whether "I" was holding my "self" aloof from it or not. Fortunately, one simply cannot *be* without being a body. One simply *is* inches of supple skin and foot after foot of gut, slosh of blood, thud of heart, lick of tongue, brain humped and folded into skull. And it is as a body that one inhabits the past and it inhabits one's body, so that, as Bachelard puts it, "the house we were born in is physically inscribed in us. It is a group of organic habits. After twenty years, in spite of all the other anonymous stairways, we would recapture the reflexes of the 'first stairway,' we would not stumble on that rather high step. . . . The word habit is too worn a word to express this passionate liaison of our bodies, which do not forget, with an unforgettable house."[15] Whether or not I permitted myself to think of my self as a body at some earlier time, I cannot deny the identity today. That identity offers my only means of entering and literally making sense of my past.

Although drawn to the autobiographical task, I do not wish however to produce an autobiography bound by the narrative conventions of temporal linearity.[16] Arranging time as a sequence of incidents aids one in establishing an alibi, say, or drawing up a list of the day's tasks. But it does not provide the means for reentering the past experientially. Its product is brittle and attenuated, a "time line," neither flexible nor massive enough to open itself to reoccupation. The past, says the philosopher Maurice Merleau-Ponty, "has its space, its paths, its nameplaces, and its monuments. Beneath the crossed but distinct orders of succession and simultaneity, beneath the train of synchronizations added onto line by line, we find a nameless network— constellations of spatial hours, of point-events." Time and space conflate: "The whole description of our landscape and the lines of our universe, and of our inner monologue, needs to be redone. Colors, sounds, and things—like Van Gogh's stars—are the focal points and radiance of being."[17]

The search for lost time, then, necessitates spatial, not merely temporal, recall. As Bachelard tells us, memory "does not record concrete duration"; rather, "we think we know ourselves in time, when all we know is a sequence of fixations in the spaces of the being's stability." Memory itself is essentially spatial: "In its countless alveoli space contains compressed time. That is what space is for."[18] We can impose a grid of time onto our memories, much as we sketch lines of latitude and longitude on a globe, a very useful device for knowing when or where we are in relation to some event or spot used as a reference point. But the memories won't yield up their freight in response. For that we have to let go of life-lines and plunge into the multiple modalities—sensory, emotional, cognitive—that have encoded the past and will release it, transformed, into the present.

To this end, I wrote a memoir—as I write most often—in the fragmented form of essays, each concentrating on a house or houses important to my growth as a woman. I sought and still seek to avoid the reassuring rigidity and muscularity I'd learned to love in the academy. To abandon the narrative structure inculcated there (exposition, complication, climax, dénouement). To refuse its critical questions (What does this mean? Why does it matter?). To embrace the past as "meaningless," as "matterless," without "worth" in an economy based on the scarcity of resources, on the fear of running out—of reasons, of memories, of precious time. To seduce the impatient reader boldly: *Here, let's take our time. We've got plenty more where it came from.* To dare to dally. These are the requisites and risks of a woman determined to experience her past—the past in which she lived as a body, which dwells in her body still—as a bower.

When we were children, we formed an enclosure of hands linked into arches and sang:

> Go in and out the window.
> Go in and out the window.
> Go in and out the window
> As you have done before.

Writing my past as a body always enacts that circle game. I invite you in because I have been schooled (not in the ivory phallus this time but in all my mothers' dim houses) in hospitality: you, my strangers, my guests. *Mi casa es su casa.*

"Writing," says Cixous, "is the passageway, the entrance, the exit, the dwelling place of the other in me."[19] Writing itself is space. It is a populated house. In the houses of my past, I often felt alone; writing about them, I am never alone. As Merleau-Ponty notes in illuminating Husserl's philosophy, "Every man [*sic*] reflecting upon his life does have the fundamental possibility of looking at it as a series of private states of consciousness, just as the white civilized adult does. But he can do so only if he forgets experiences which bestride this everyday and serial time, or reconstitutes them in a way which caricatures them. The fact that we die alone does not imply that we live alone."[20] I cannot be without the other. I cannot be without you.

I cannot write my self without writing you, my other. I don't believe literally that in writing my "life" I am writing yours as well. On the contrary, I feel certain I am not. You didn't get bitten on the foot by red ants when you were four, did you? You didn't sing "Lullay, Thou Little Tiny Child" in the fourth-grade Christmas pageant? Your baby bunny wasn't chewed up and swallowed, hind legs last, by your Irish setter, Pegeen? You don't eat the same thing for breakfast every morning of your life? You're not still scared of the dark? These are my details. And heaven knows I have enough trouble getting them straight without keeping track of yours as well.

In fact, this is one of the problems that dog me in autobiographical work: I can never get the details right to the satisfaction of everyone who shows up in the telling. Merleau-Ponty comments that "all action and all love are haunted by the expectation of an account which will transform them into their truth."[21] My mother's in particular. Each time I complete a project, she'd like to check it over to make sure I've told things as they "really" happened this time, having missed the mark mightily in some earlier book. Others who find themselves presented in my work no doubt wish the same. But the past, that ramshackle structure, is a fabrication. I make it up as I go along. The only promise I can state about its "reality" is that I "really" remember (reembody? flesh out anew?) the details I record; that is, I don't deliberately invent any of them.

On the whole, however, I don't seek historical accuracy either. Instead, I try, in Merleau-Ponty's words, "to give the past not a survival, which is the hypocritical form of forgetfulness, but a new life, which is the noble form of memory."[22] What my mother, for one, will have to remember is that, as Sidonie Smith puts it, "the autobiographical text becomes a narrative artifice, privileging a presence, or identity, that does not exist outside language. Given the very nature of language, embedded in the text lie alternative or deferred identities that constantly subvert any pretentions of truthfulness."[23] In these terms, I can't even tell my own truth, much less anyone else's. I can only settle the problem in the manner of Clément's sorceress: "she is true because she believes her own lies."[24]

And yet, in a deeper sense of the word, I hope that I speak truthfully about all our lives. Because I think that my "story," though intensely personal, is not at all singular. Beneath its idiosyncrasies lie vast strata of commonality, communality. It is not, at that level, an original tale. To quote Merleau-Ponty again,

> The individual drama takes place among *roles* which are already inscribed in the total institutional structure, so that from the beginning of his life the child proceeds . . . to a deciphering of meanings which from the outset generalizes his own drama into a drama of his culture . . . Consequently, there is not a single detail of his most individual history which does not contribute something to

that personal significance he will manifest when . . . he finally comes to the point of reversing the relationship and . . . converting even the most secret aspects of his experience into culture. . . . These reversals, these "metamorphoses," . . . this way that cultural time and space roll up on themselves, and this perpetual overdetermination of human events which . . . makes *every other person another ourself* for us—all these things become conceivable or even visible to the philosophical attitude alone.[25]

And, I would add, they inform the autobiographical attitude, at least for the feminist autobiographer, writing out of a sense of connectedness. I don't see how anyone engaged in self-representation can fail to recognize in this self, constructed as it is in language, all the others whom the writing self shelters. The not-me dwells here in the me. We are one, and more-than-one. Our stories utter one another.

"Thus, very quickly," writes Bachelard, "at the very first word, at the first poetic overture, the reader who is 'reading a room' leaves off reading and starts to think of some place in his own past. You would like to tell everything about your room. You would like to interest the reader in yourself, whereas you have unlocked a door to daydreaming. The values of intimacy are so absorbing that the reader has ceased to read your room: he sees his own again."[26] If I do my job, the books I write vanish before your eyes. I invite you into the house of my past, and the threshold you cross leads you into your own.

part three

Notes

from

the

Field

The Literature of Personal Disaster

a few days before Christmas 1990, hunched on the edge of a folding cot with my laptop computer on a little table drawn up to my knees, I wrote compulsively, hour after hour, as though capturing my world in detail could defer its end. After every few words, I glanced across the top of the screen at my husband, slit and stitched up and webbed in plastic tubing, so wasted and waxy that I had to keep reminding myself: *This is George. You know him. You have loved him for almost thirty years.* "I suppose there are millions of us at this very moment in just the same pain," I tapped on the keys. "Why do I feel so *singular?*"

Yes, millions keeping bedside vigils, whispering as I whispered over and over, *Come back! Don't leave me! I need you!*, each of us trapped in this profound and irrational solitude, as though walls of black glass had dropped on every side, shutting out the light, deadening all sound but the loved one's morphine-drugged breathing: I was not, in truth, alone. Was it that intuition which had driven me before, and would goad me again, to write intimately about illness, disability, and death? And does the same suspicion provoke others to tell their stories—so much like mine, so absolutely their own? Are we all groping for one another through our separate darks?

Because my books have dealt candidly with my own multiple sclerosis, suicidal depression, and agoraphobia, as well as my husband's melanoma, I am frequently asked to review or endorse works that belong to a distinct though largely unrecognized sub-genre I've come to call, only half-facetiously, the Literature of Personal Disaster. Knowing from painful experience what can happen when one's work falls to a reviewer so unempathic that he wishes not only that one had written some other book but also that one had lived some other life, I'm willing enough to read, on their own terms, first-hand accounts of AIDS (Elizabeth Cox's *Thanksgiving: An AIDS Journal*), freak accidents (Andre Dubus's *Broken Vessels*) and illnesses (Molly Haskell's *Love and Other Infectious Diseases*), manic depression (Kate Millett's *The Loony-Bin Trip*), childbirth gone awry (Anne Finger's *Past Due*), cancer (Susan Kenney's *In Another Country* and *Sailing*), polio (Leonard Kriegel's *Falling Into Life*), deafness (Carol Glickfeld's *Useful Gifts*), stroke (May Sarton's *After the Stroke*), widowhood (Rebecca Rice's *A Time To Mourn*), to name only a few. These are serious works of fiction and nonfiction, not the print equivalents of the sensational sagas touted by "Geraldo" or "A Current Affair," and they warrant my attention, if not always my affection.

I consider reviewing a professional obligation, and ordinarily I take the books assigned to me rather than select them myself. Thus, I did not choose to be the kind of connoisseur of catastrophe I have gradually become. But what of other readers, the ones a publisher's marketing staff must have in mind when they give an editor the nod for a journal delineating a mother's slow wasting from pancreatic cancer (Le Anne Schreiber's *Midstream*) or the remembrance of a beloved husband, newly dead (Madeleine L'Engle's *Two-Part Invention*)? If, as I have read, something like a thousand new titles are published each week, what do the bookmongers believe will draw readers to these two? Sorrow? Curiosity? What are they supposed to find there? Solace? Reassurance? Sheer relief that, however wretched their own lives may seem, others are worse?

In short: Why do I, and others like me, write this stuff? Why does anybody read it? (Or, to put the matter more cynically but no doubt more accurately, why does anybody think anybody else is going to pay good money to read it?) And what, if anything, happens when they do?

In *A Nation of Victims*, a book more wrong-hearted than wrong-headed, which could have been written only by a well-educated young Euro-American male who appears in his jacket photo to be in the pink of condition, Charles J. Sykes complains that, U.S. society having "degenerated into a community of insistent sufferers," our "National Anthem has become The Whine."[1] If so, then one might reasonably expect the works I'm writing about, founded as they are in pain and loss, to form an analogous National Literature. But in truth, virtually no writer I've encountered has sounded more aggrieved than Mr. Sykes himself. Sad, yes. Frightened, yes. Furious, yes. But almost never plaintive.

The true victim—the person set apart from ordinary human intercourse by temporary or permanent misfortune— has little enough time and even less energy for sniveling. Illness and death, whether one's own or a beloved's, take *work*, and I'm not using the word metaphorically. There are hands to be held and basins to be emptied and upper lips to be kept stiff. One has to husband one's resources. Self-pity simply doesn't provide an adequate motive for expending precious effort to write about the ordeal. But the work, tough as it is, feels singularly instructive, as though one were taking up a severe and rather odd new discipline, spelunking, perhaps, something that draws one through the stink of bat guano toward an unfathomable abyss. It pricks all one's senses.

The impulse, at least for someone of a writerly persuasion, is not to bemoan this condition but to remark it in detail. Initially, one's motives for translating happenstance into acts of language may be quite private. Catastrophe tends to be composed not of a monolithic event but of a welter of little incidents, many of which bear no apparent relationship to one another, and language, in ordering these into recognizable patterns, counteracts disorientation and disintegration. This process of making sense of a flood of random data also produces the impression—generally quite groundless—of control, which may save one's sanity even though it can't save one's own or anyone else's life.

These therapeutic results provide ample reason for keeping a personal journal, but they don't account for the penchant of some writers (and most of the words I have in mind were written by people who would have been writing *something* anyway) for transforming intimate experience into public artifact. Some may share my aesthetic drive: to transmute dross—my own hastening physical deterioration, my husband's wretched, retching progress through chemotherapy—into lapidary reality. And some may find, as I have done, that they thereby write their way into better behavior than they believed themselves capable of. I am forever publishing brave statements that I must then make good on if I am to be a woman of my word.

I can't always do so, of course, but sometimes I can. And since I possess no extraordinary existential gifts, I assume that you can, too. You will need to, I know. All of us who write out of calamity know this before all else: there is nothing exceptional about our lives, however these may differ in their particulars. What we can offer you, when the time comes, is companionship in a common venture. It's not a lot, I know, but it may come in handy. The narrator of personal disaster, I think, wants not to whine, not to boast, but to comfort. As one of the sufferers interviewed in Cheri Register's *Living with Chronic Illness*[2] points out, it is possible to be *both* sick *and* happy. This good news, once discovered, demands to be shared.

This underlying drive to console may account for the fact that more women than men seem attracted to the genre and that the works of women tend to be more intimate and immediate than those of men. This gender difference is not essential but circumstantial: women have traditionally been accorded social permission both to suffer and to mitigate suffering, especially messy suffering, the kind involving fevers, excreta, compresses, and nursery puddings. Men, by contrast, have been supposed to pretend that nothing hurts or frightens them, not the bully's rabbit punches on the playground, not the black tumor gnawing at the entrails, *nothing*, and to sneer at pain and terror in others. Choosing to speak publicly about affliction is risky for both, but for different reasons: for the woman, because the behavior (public utterance) is culturally impermissible; for the man, because the condition (physical or mental weakness) is proscribed. Clearly, the woman who undertakes to publish a book about her miseries, or about anything else, has already decided to transgress, at whatever cost, the taboo on female speech; thus, she has resolved the crucial issue before beginning her project. But a man, who is expected to speak publicly but not to expose his infirmities, may have to struggle with this conflict of (self)interest in the writing itself.

The approved resolution to his problem is to distance the authorial subject from the suffering subject. The author— highly intelligent, perceptive, above all in control—may then scrutinize and explain and interpret pain without ever appearing to fall victim to it. This use of intellect to divorce self from experience may account for the peculiar deadness of a book on madness like William Styron's *Darkness Visible* when contrasted with the third, "depressed" section of *The Loony-Bin Trip*, which forces the reader to pace Kate Millet's narrow, grimy kitchen along with her as she subsists on soda crackers and coffee, unable to write, unable to speak, her attention contracted to a single point: "Oneself. In danger."[3]

That intellectualization is not a strictly gender-bound coping strategy is made clear by Susan Sontag's brilliant but icy *Illness As Metaphor*, which bears no trace of the author's personal encounter with cancer. I don't condemn nonpersonal analysis; on the contrary, I for one need *Illness As Metaphor* to be exactly as it is. But the drawback to an approach like Styron's—openly self-referential yet without intimacy—is that it also distances the reader from an experience she or he may have no other means for understanding. I've *been* mad in just the way Styron has, and even I couldn't figure out from his book what such a state feels like.

Which happens to be fine with me, since I already know. (Not that great, no matter what poets of disaster like Sylvia Plath and Anne Sexton suggest.) But what of the woman who wrote to me after her lover had shot herself to death? She didn't need a description of depression (she was a psychiatrist) but a means of fathoming suicidal despair. She needed to enter and endure it with me. Those writers who seek to console and hearten must make themselves and their anguish wholly transparent, revealing not illness as metaphor but illness as illness, in order to persuade the skeptical reader, through the very writing, that survival (at least till the last page) is possible.

With the exception of the strictly private journal, which lies outside any literary discussion unless its author later decides to change its status, the sense of isolation I mentioned earlier figures powerfully in the writer's impulse to record calamitous events intending to make them public. Publication of any sort is an intrinsically social act, "I" having no

129

reason to speak aloud unless I posit "you" there listening; but your presence is especially vital if I am seeking not to disclose the economic benefits of fish farming in Zaïre, or to recount the imaginary tribulations of an adulterous doctor's wife in nineteenth-century France, but to reconnect my self—now so utterly transformed by events unlike any I've experienced before as to seem a stranger even to myself—to the human community.

The "you" required by such an "I" must be unusually vivid and available, I know as a writer. That is, in writing I construct an ideal reader possessing these characteristics. But I don't expect real readers to share them. Real readers, in fact, puzzle me a bit, the way women puzzled Freud, and I'm terrifically grateful to the ones who write and tell me what they want, which tends to be advice (sometimes), sympathy (often), and (every now and then) the chance to give me pieces of their minds, some of these more palatable than others. Many want simply to thank me for putting their feelings into words. These voices, lending materiality to my readerly ideal, transform monologue into intercourse.

When I take up the role of reader myself, I sense a discrepancy between my own readers, both imagined and actual, who are generally smart, sensitive, and sympathetic, and those some published have in mind for their releases. (Or do they have readers, as distinct from consumers, in mind at all?) I don't read the most disastrous disaster narratives, I'm sure, since these never make it as far as the reviewer's desk. Only once have I had to tell a publisher that not only would I not endorse the book he sent me, if I were he I wouldn't even publish it. (He did, and went belly up not long afterward, which gave me less satisfaction than I would have anticipated.) I read nothing written in pop-psyche-speak, on principle, and I lack the background to comment on books, good or bad, dealing with sexual or substance abuse. All the same, too much of what I do read is poorly conceived, clumsily written, and carelessly edited.

Although bad books are published in every genre, I know, I mind these more, perhaps because I feel a certain defensiveness about personal disaster as an authentic literary subject. As people with disabilities who were once shuttered by shame and superstition move out into productive roles in society, and as society is enriched by their participation, we will all benefit from the increase in awareness and information their works provide; and surely we can all use the solace derived from knowing that the grief and fury we feel when "bitten by bad nature," as Sylvia Plath puts it,[4] has been endured by at least one other person. We must take care, however, not to condescend subtly to such authors by lowering the literary standards to which we hold them out of a cynical or sentimental misreading of readers' needs and expectations.

What, if not misplaced pity, prompted an editor to accept for publication a manuscript in the first chapter of which a psychiatrist likens the challenge of psychoanalyzing the raving paranoiac who has just showed up in his tastefully accoutred Central Park office to "trying to make par on a long and winding hole where you cannot see the green as you tee off." The entire book turns out to be just as shallow as its founding metaphor would suggest. Did the editor consider writers about madness too inept to produce literature of quality? Did he believe that only voyeuristic or prurient readers would be drawn to a book on such a topic, and that they merited whatever they got? Less cynically, did he regard schizophrenia as so urgent a subject that the usual standards ought to be waived in order to broadcast as much information as possible?

Although in some instances (I wonder whether AIDS might be a contemporary case), such a documentary function might justify publication, it cannot by itself make books in this genre work as literature. It's not enough to feel bad nature's bite: to find yourself, having stopped to help two stranded motorists, catapulted by a speeding car into the night, from which you wake to a new life without the use of your legs; to flounder about, baffled and bitter, for some way to prepare your young children for their father's death; to drag yourself, in an ill and aging body, from bed to desk and back again until you weep and wish for death. These are central situations in some of the best work being done in this genre, but by themselves they're merely horrific, not redemptive. Misery, no matter how mysterious and poignant, is not enough to make a book, and if an editor and the marketing strategists who drive editorial decisions think it is, somebody (or preferably a lot of somebodies) has to tell them otherwise.

The trick, with this as with any genre, is to satisfy its requirements while escaping its confines. The writing about personal disaster which functions as literature tends not to be "about" disaster at all. That is, whatever adversity provides the grounds for the project must be embedded in a context both enigmatic and elaborate: the insistent everyday world. For this reason, perhaps, writers already experienced in other genres are apt to accomplish most in this one. The works of the writers I have in mind transcend their separate ordeals to speak generally, and generously, of the human condition.

Andre Dubus, a critically acclaimed writer of short fiction, was indeed struck by a car and crippled permanently in 1986. But *Broken Vessels* is extraordinary not because it depicts physical and emotional trauma but because it demonstrates tacitly, by collecting essays written between 1977 and 1990, the spiritual maturation that suffering can force: "After the dead are buried, and the maimed have left the hospitals and started their new lives, after the physical pain of grief has become, with time, a permanent wound in the soul, a sorrow that will last as long as the body does, after the horrors become nightmares and sudden daylight memories, then comes the transcendent and common bond of human suffering, and with that comes forgiveness, and with forgiveness comes love. . . ."[5] The life that leads one to this point can no longer be termed in any sense disastrous.

Susan Kenney, who has chosen to treat the issues raised by her husband's cancer in fictional form, delineates a similar progress toward sympathetic wisdom as her central characters, Sara and Phil, move ambivalently and ambiguously toward Phil's death. One of the great virtues of both *In Another Country* and *Sailing* lies in Kenney's eye and ear for the comic in even quite grisly situations, as when Phil, in the throes of chemotherapy's nausea, performs spectacularly in front of a traffic cop, thereby sparing Sara a speeding ticket. The memory of this scene buoyed me through many a gastric eruption during George's chemotherapy. The truth is that those of us in calamitous circumstances laugh a good deal, not just because Norman Cousins has told us to,

133

though his was excellent advice, but because funny things go on happening to people no matter what. Kenney's capacity for capturing life's clutter—the way cancer has to fit in among children's tantrums and Christmas shopping and the pressures of work and the death of the old dog—shows suffering in its proper scale, not inconsequential, by any means, but not insurmountable either.

Like Dubus and Kenney, May Sarton captures and celebrates the commonplace, in her poems and novels but especially in her journals, of which *Endgame* is the most recent. Over the years, she has drawn her audience into her world—the cats, the lilacs and daylilies and tree peonies, the bottles of Vouvray and champagne, and always the dogged work of a prolific writer—so meticulously that when I was given the chance to call on her last summer, I stepped into a landscape already familiar, salt meadow joining the yellow house with the sweep of the sea. There I met at last the woman who had been teaching me what to love about solitude, about company, for years. She gave me chilled wine and *gaufrettes* and one white rose from her garden.

As Sarton's health has failed, wearing her to translucency, infirmity has surfaced, gradually and naturally, as a major theme in her recent work. In permitting it to emerge instead of painting it over, she communicates a harsh lesson: aging is the one disaster that, if we escape all others, will claim us in the end. As luck and the actuarial tables would have it, most of "us" will be women, many of whom, having endured the grievous loss of a life partner, will suffer both the lack of "the tangible 'we' when two people live together in amity" and loneliness "in essence for the *self*,"[6] the former resilient and responsive self, who now creeps crab-like across the ice to the car for yet another trip to the doctor who will never again make her well. Eventually, each will say, "I want to die, there's no doubt about that. When you have as much pain as I have and there's no way out you *do* want to die, if you're as old as I am. . . . There is that hope that someday, while you're asleep, the old heart will stop beating."[7]

Yet, in spite of her admission that now "everything hurts," Sarton casts aside "fantasies of suicide as a way out of the constant chronic pain. . . . I feel one must have one's death, one must not make one's own death. One must let death come when the time has come." In the meantime, she writes, not so much about being old and ill as about what matters moment by moment: not a "really appallingly frail and old-looking woman" but the person within, "seeing an awful lot, being aware of an awful lot"—a friend's thick, savory soup, and Pierrot the Himalayan, who looks "like a Roman emperor in cat form," and the house filled with dewy pale pink roses, purple anemones, white and lavender tulips, blue asters. . . .[8] These are books about going on. All the way. To our common destination.

To which none of us wants to go ignorant and alone. Hence, into the dark, we write.

The Writer's Thin Skin and Faint Heart

Oh to forget all this and write—as I must tomorrow.

—VIRGINIA WOOLF, *A Writer's Diary*

Recently I took up Virginia Woolf's *A Writer's Diary* again. I had not reread it in full for the better part of a decade, nor did I intend to do so this time, merely to browse and take a few notes. But the voices of writers with whom you feel intimate can be hard to resist, especially if they speak of matters you haven't heeded in earlier readings. The first few times I pored over this diary, as an aspiring writer, I attended to Woolf's descriptions of the processes entailed in producing a book. I believed myself incapable of such a feat, and my reading did little to change my mind. I had to do it at first by accident, composing individual poems and later individual essays, only afterward recognizing that the way these informed and played off one another constituted bookness.

Later, when a publisher offered what was for me an enormous advance on the basis of an eight-page book proposal, I was terrified. The publisher clearly expected something, but I hadn't the least idea whether I could make up a book from scratch and on purpose. It turned out that I could, and also that finding out this truth about myself had virtually no impact on the terror. Writing is not, alas, like riding a bicycle: it does not get easier with practice. Every time I took out a yellow legal-size pad and fountain pen, and now when I turn on the computer and stare at the blank screen, I'm petrified again: *this* time nothing will happen, or something will happen so ruinous as to defy repair, so safer just to turn the computer back off and reread Virginia Woolf instead, to whom nothing deplorable ever happened while a pen was in her hand, even when she was only lamenting the difficulty of finding a reliable cook.

Nevertheless, I take up *A Writer's Diary* only outside those hours reserved for the hypnotic fits of ague—now icy with blank anxiety, now flushed to fulmination, now, briefly, steady and clearheaded—I know as writing. And I find it in some ways a different book from the one I remembered, just as I am not the woman who first sought initiation into the mysteries of a writer's life. Now I live that life, and on the whole I like it well enough—no, let me not be mealy-mouthed, on the whole I am enraptured by it—but some bits of it, I've been chagrinned to discover, prick me bloody. And Woolf is there, her ambivalences anticipating my own.

At the heart of these lies the matter of exposure. "Is the

137

time coming," Woolf wonders, "when I can endure to read my own writing in print without blushing—shivering and wishing to take cover?"[1] Typesetting transmutes the work-as-one-knows-it, an intimate space in which one has sheltered, often all but alone, for months or years, into a theatre which anybody with a checkbook or a library card may enter at will. The sense of intrusion is a paradoxical response, of course, since publication was the point all along. The writing process is essentially transactional. At some moment, the writer has got to let her work go into the hands of at least one other in order for it to become "written" at all. And that other may . . . oh, God alone knows what that other may do, but it hardly bears contemplating. If the very thought of taking off all your clothes in the middle of the Washington Mall during a school holiday makes you blush, you haven't even begun to dream what it feels like to publish a book.

The fact that I am by nature reclusive strikes people as incongruous with the personal candor I display in my books. But frankness itself functions as a kind of screen, more effective in some ways than the legendary obsession with privacy of J. D. Salinger or Thomas Pynchon, say, because it deflects rather than kindles curiosity. *If she tells me all this*, a reader is likely to reason, *what can be left to say?* Behind this public Nancy, the introvert curls up with her books and computer, two cats and a corgi her only company, for hours every day.

This solitude is broken by letters and an occasional telephone call. Now and then, these can be a little peculiar, offering me advice about my dental work, for example, but generally they are well-intentioned and welcome. People who despise your work—like the man who, his wife reported solemnly, hurled my book *Plaintext* across the room after reading only one essay—are unlikely to trouble themselves to call or write to tell you so. Nevertheless, such are the quirks of the human heart, the handful of negative responses are the ones that have lodged there, stinging like nettles sometimes for years. When I get one, my impulse is to race through bookshops and libraries, hauling all remaining copies off the shelves, telephone my editor to halt the release of whatever book is in production, and never show another word to a soul. I cannot, I have learned, prevent myself from writing, but I might, through self-censorship, avoid ever giving offense—and receiving chastisement—again.

139

Reviews are both more and less problematic than letters. They can be every bit as bizarre, like the one by a woman who felt, in reading *Plaintext*, as though I'd laced her food with broken glass. God knows they create more anxiety (over whether the book will be reviewed at all and then whether it will have been read intelligently, if not reviewed favorably) and, because they are public, more embarrassment as well. But the very fact that they can be anticipated robs them of a cruel letter's power to stun. An occasional reviewer leaps at the license to savage and ridicule, but most work thoughtfully, if not always in a blaze of insight, not just because they know that their turn will come soon enough but because the writing profession tends to attract perfectionists who want to get words right. I undertake every review I write in good faith, and I choose to believe that others do, too. I can accept quite a negative critique if my work has been handled respectfully.

But I'll never like disapproval, no matter how fairly couched, I suspect, since "the worst of writing is that one depends so much upon praise,"[2] and the praise counts for so little in relation to even a whisper of blame. To be "dashed" may always have been the most "bracing treatment" for Woolf, making her style more "definite and outspoken,"[3] but it mires me in sadness and self-doubt. I'm especially aware of having been tried and found wanting every year at about the same time—roughly January through March—when I hit a bad patch quite different from the sorts Woolf talks about. It's of my own making, to be sure, but that doesn't make me like it any better. Probably worse.

A few months beforehand, in a ritual at once hopeful and masochistic, I've applied for a handful of writing fellowships. These, offered locally (by the Tucson/Pima Arts Council), at the state level (by the Arizona Commission on the Arts), federally (by the National Endowment for the Arts), or privately (by the Guggenheim Foundation), provide amounts of money from a couple of thousand to twenty thousand dollars or more, not inconsiderable sums for all but the most popular writers, promising periods from a month to a year or more of unobstructed writing time. Preparing the applications, which require forms and multiple copies of writing samples, is both laborious and expensive, but I don't mind the hours or the postage so much as the gloomy precognition (I've been at this for years now) that I've set myself up once again for the next winter's letters: "We regret to inform you . . ."

Of course, no matter how meticulously and gracefully

I've prepared my work, no matter how attentively and sympathetically the judge(s) read it, it has only a slender chance of winning any competition. That's the nature of competition, to create a vast number of losers in proportion to the number of winners. I know that. I also know that personal animus is unlikely to underlie my rejections (in fact, many competitions are judged blind). Why then do I find them so painful?

Invariably, as I unfold the rejection letter, disappointment and shame explode in my gut and for days I can't draw a full breath. I feel spurned, degraded, hollowed out, tossed aside. Something more grievous than the withholding of funds haunts me here: the scene of (failed) seduction. My imagination, given only a form letter to feed on, freely invents a judge—always a "real" writer of impeccable discernment—who, flicking his eyes over my pages, curls his lip in just the way my ninth-grade science teacher must have done on receiving my anonymous professions of passion, and perhaps even hoots once at my pretensions as he tosses them onto the rising refuse heap. Having been a judge myself, I know that these behaviors don't go on at every site of rejection, but we're not talking reason here. We're talking the death of the heart.

I'm not sure such an event is good for me, good for my body. It's certainly not good for my writing, which stops altogether, frozen by insecurity and, as my physical condition deteriorates, a kind of bitter self-pity I despise. ("We hope you'll apply for funding in the future," said one recent rejection letter, as though the loser would assuredly endure to grab for the brass ring one year after the next, forever. Yeah, sure.) Maybe I'm the only person to feel this way. I don't know. In all the writers' conferences and workshops and social gatherings I've attended, I've never heard the matter spoken of aloud, and so I suppose it falls, like most instances of emotional vulnerability, outside the realm of polite discourse. But if failing in competition has such agonizing consequences for me, I might do well to remove myself from it.

That's also the nature of competition: to create not just loss but the pain of loss. The thrill of victory, too, of course, for some happy few. But does the one justify the other? Does the one even justify itself? Is competition the right paradigm for evaluating and rewarding art (or anything else)? Is there an alternative to the competitive model? After all, the whole world seems a maelstrom of testosterone—what's one more contest in the flow? Woolf, who recognized the connection between privilege and war, and who turned down even the prime minister's offer to recommend her for the Companion of Honour, is explicit here: "You must refuse all methods of advertising merit, and hold that ridicule, obscurity and censure are preferable, for psychological reasons, to fame and praise. Directly badges, orders or degrees are offered you, fling them back in the giver's face."[4] Accepting her premise as I do, should I too cultivate a "philosophy of anonymity"[5] and refrain from entering contests? Should I refuse to be a judge? I'd like to flee the moral and emotional ambiguities here. But I'd better pick through them, because they matter to my health as a writer.

Oh, but you're just a poor loser, I can hear confirmed competitors assure me. *All you need is to win, and then you'll like contests well enough.* In fact, I have won, more than once, but those victories have created quandaries of their own. My misgivings began to grow, on the weedy bottom where all such disturbances take root, when I won one of the 1984 Western States Book Awards. I was in rough shape at the time: grieving that my daughter's departure for college left me with only two cats for female company, one of them nuttier than a fruitcake (which she rather resembled); not just then in love with my husband; burnt out on teaching and nervously beginning a new administrative job; a bitter year away from finishing my dissertation. Even my aged Volvo station wagon had stopped functioning reliably. Under these conditions, I wrote in my journal earlier on the day I would receive word:

> I catch myself fantasizing that I've won and give myself a mental slap. . . . When I was young I permitted myself fantasies and enjoyed them fully, but now I know that they won't be fulfilled and so I strike them down, fearing that they'll only make my disappointment the more poignant, though I don't know that they really do. The victory of realism/cynicism. I am denied not only the joy of winning but even the joy of dreaming about winning. And still secretly I want . . . desperately, desperately to win, so that my disappointment, fed by fantasies or not—will be crushing.

When my publisher told me I had won the prize for poetry, I was pierced by joy more perfect than I have felt before or since. And in the next instant, perhaps because I knew one of them or only because I'd been such a one myself, I thought of all the others who wouldn't feel it this time. I was then, and remain, haunted by the losers. I bought my happiness—and it was real, has continued to be real—at their expense. I did not, of course, wish to relinquish the award. I simply wanted all of us to win. "What a discovery that would be—a system that did not shut out."[6]

Although winning feels infinitely more delicious than losing, I've noticed a couple of queer things about it. One is that, once I've won, the "prize" loses some of its cachet, as though it couldn't really have been very significant if even the likes of me could achieve it. And the second, which may be related, is that it never suffices. For a while I experience a "hiatus of desire," such as the Western States Book Award brought, in which "I can still think of lots of things I want, of course, most involving scads of money . . . but for the moment they have no hold on my happiness." But before long I want again the lovely rush success brings, in larger quantities, and more often. Like Woolf, "I think the nerve of pleasure easily becomes numb."[7] I've never been addicted to any substance but nicotine, for which my desire does not seem to escalate as it is said to do with heroin or cocaine, but I wonder whether I'm a success junky and whether, as May Sarton once speculated, "in the very long run any success devours—and perhaps also corrupts."[8] With infantile insatiability, I crave *all* the fellowships, *all* the awards, *all* the praise, heaped glittering around me like a dragon's hoard, and my greed unsettles and shames me.

Since the odds of losing are so great, however, most of us get more practice at being a loser than a winner. I, for one, do not like to lose, and I don't know anyone else who does, either, but I've had ample opportunity to discover that some responses to defeat suit me better than others do. A few years ago, when the list of winners sent along with my rejection letter from the NEA included a close friend whose struggle to establish herself as a poet had been more exhausting than rewarding, I went immediately to the telephone.

"How splendid that you got an NEA!" I told her. "Oh, I wish I'd gotten one, too!"

She laughed, and we gleefully discussed her plans for the money. A couple of days later, she thanked me for that call. Mine had been, she said, the only "generous" response to her achievement. In fact, a mutual acquaintance, a poet far better known than either of us, running into her at the university where they both taught, had asked her airily whether he hadn't heard some news about her recently— something to do with an award, maybe? . . .

"Oh, for God's sake, Cynthia!" I said. "You know he knows perfectly well it was an NEA. He applied too, I'll bet, and didn't get one!" It was too soon for anyone but recipients of the NEA's letter to have heard the results. "And why shouldn't I rejoice with you? It's not as though your winning diminishes me. On the contrary!" Crushed though I was to have been refused again, at least a fellowship had gone to someone I loved whose work, wholly unlike my own, I admired. If this constitutes generosity (which I doubt), then call me Lady Bountiful. The plain fact is that I made myself happier by cheering Cynthia's success from the position of her friend and reader than that poet made himself, as her competitor, by begrudging it.

Not that I can't be grumpy in my turn. Just a few weeks ago I was notified that having been given a "merit award" in a local fellowship competition, I was invited to a reception for the honorees. Well, hell, I thought, if they're not going to give me any money, why should I put myself out to drink tea from a styrofoam cup and eat gooey cake and make artsy chitchat? The truth was that I felt not merely disappointed but mortified to have not-quite-lost in a field of only forty-seven. That's the trouble with honorable mentions: they let everyone know you applied and didn't win.

"Do I have to go to this thing?" I asked my husband.

"An award is an award, Nancy," he said, ignoring my pout. "I think you should go." (One should always live with someone who will fill in for one's better nature when one's better nature goes on holiday.) Afterward, I was glad George and I had gone and lent our support to the winners in literature, all of whom I knew, and the small local arts organization who sponsored the competition. I hope the mean spirits of the merit award recipients who didn't show up stung and throbbed! (When one has narrowly missed behaving badly, smugness tends to creep in.)

Beneath all my qualms about winning—affection, fair judgment, public honor, even money—lies the question at the core of my life as a writer: "Do I ever write . . . for my own eye? If not, for whose eye?"[9] Whose opinion unquestionably frets me so—the "ideal observer," my own "true self," some severe professor, long-suffering Mother who says I always get my tales a little wrong? Perhaps you can imagine a writer so dismissive of readers that he or she doesn't care how they respond, or at least pretends to dismiss them so as to appear not to care, but I cannot. Without readers—whether fans or reviewers or judges—I do not feel myself to exist. My writing arises out of erotic impulse toward an other: it is an act of love. And I want terribly to be loved in return, as a sign that I have loved well enough.

The intense drive to captivate readers might provoke professional jealousy, in the way that possessive love can trigger sexual jealousy, but I haven't found this to be the case. Accolades have gone to writing I consider inferior to my own, true, but also to writing—Joan Didion's essays spring immediately to mind, and Mary Oliver's poems— clearly superior; and in both cases, since I recognize hierarchizing as a cultural tic rather than a reflection of intrinsic merit, these judgments don't much interest me. We each do the work we have to do. I wish I could have written, in the middle of a poem about a bear in spring,

> There is only one question:
> how to love this world.[10]

But I don't feel jealous of the woman who wrote those lines, and I certainly don't covet her readers, as though there were only so many of them to go around, as though the readers of Mary Oliver are somehow "lost" to me. Her readers (including me) are hers, and mine are mine, and some—this would be best of all—may read us both.

My use of personal pronouns here is not intended to be proprietary. Rather, it signals a change I've begun to observe in the way I relate to the construct "reader," which I can only describe as the growing sense that the "one" to whom I speak has moved in with me, deep within me, and we live together in a radical collaborative intimacy concentrated on the task at hand. Not that I no longer want or need or love readers "out there" but that I can simply enjoy them without leaning on them for reassurance and satisfaction. Whatever the infant in me screeches, I *have* had enough grateful letters, enough good reviews, enough awards. What I have not yet had enough of is work. Like Woolf, though ten years later than she, "there's no doubt in my mind that I have found out how to begin (at 40) to say something in my own voice; and that interests me so that I feel I can go ahead without praise."[11] Some readers, I can now trust, will respond to my voice, and because I am a word-of-mouth writer, they will pass me on to daughters and mothers, childhood friends, lovers, students, some of whom will love my words and others of whom will hurl them across the room. Admiration will make me happy and disapproval will make me miserable and I'll go on working anyway.

In fact, in the course of composing this essay, I received this year's Guggenheim rejection. Once again, the grief of defeat washing over me left me gasping: *You're no good, no good, no good, no good, no good. . . .*: "meretricious, mediocre, a humbug," Woolf echoes.[12] And the first review of my new book just came out, by chance a good one, but who knows what derision the next few weeks will bring. . . . Yet my anguish and anxiety seem a little less overwhelming this time. Have woe and the dread of woe worn callouses on my soul? Perhaps. But other sources for my resilience seem more plausible, in particular the fact that since I'm writing about them, public exposure and competitive loss act as sources not merely of raw pain but also of raw material: I can put them to use. Through language I have transformed some of the truly insupportable elements of my life—realities far worse than a bad review or a fellowship denied—and the trick appears to have worked again. I'm engaged more by writing than by losing.

Above all, as for Woolf, "it's the writing, not the being read, that excites me,"[13] and I've already begun to dream the next endeavor. Just a couple of weeks before the dreaded letter arrived, I was pondering whether the decimation of a lively lizard settlement in the rubble of bricks outside my studio door might correlate with the prodigious girth of Spanky, the young tabby tom next door. As I grow weaker and wearier, I spend more of my life in such rapt attention to the infinitesimal. Suddenly, blinking out into the late-winter sunlight, searching vainly for a scuffle in the weeds or the flick of a tiny tail between shadow and shadow, I felt a tug: to delineate the spatial and temporal contours of the site where I and others like me conduct our lives, right beneath the noses, so to speak, of the robust. Down here crouched my topic for next year's Guggenheim proposal: "Waist-High in the World: (Re)Constructing (Dis)Ability."

Nothing thickens a writer's skin and strengthens her heart like the sudden vision of a new venture, and this one will be dramatically new, written using voice-activated equipment now that my fingers are too weak to push a pen or punch a keyboard. I could feel myself tear free from anxious ambition: "Just *give up*," as May Sarton reports, "and be happily and fruitfully my unfashionable, unsuccessful yet productive self. Let the bones shine in the dark after I am dead. For now it does not matter."[14] For now what matters is that I have an idea and, perhaps, the means and the nerve to carry it out. With my voice, of all things, I may write a proposal. With my voice I may go on, fellowship or no, to write a book. Stranger things have happened.

Notes

PRELUDE

1. Carolyn Heilbrun, *Writing a Woman's Life* (New York: W. W. Norton, 1988), p. 37.

2. Alice A. Jardine, *Gynesis: Configurations of Woman and Modernity* (Ithaca: Cornell University Press, 1985), p. 42.

3. Heilbrun, *Writing a Woman's Life*, p. 46.

4. Jane Tompkins, "Me and My Shadow," in *Gender and Theory: Dialogues on Feminist Criticism*, ed. Linda Kaufman (New York: Basil Blackwell, 1989), p. 127.

VOICE LESSONS

1. For we (mis)speak only out of irredeemable loss—loss of the infantile "imaginary harmony with the mother and the world," in the words of Toril Moi (*Sexual/Textual Politics: Feminist Literary*

Theory [London and New York: Routledge, 1988], p. 101).

2. Rosemary Radford Ruether, *Disputed Questions: On Being a Christian* (New York: Orbis Books, 1989), p. 128.

BODY AT WORK

1. Jacques Lacan, *Feminine Sexuality*, ed. Juliet Mitchell and Jacqueline Rose, tr. Jacqueline Rose (New York: W. W. Norton, 1982), p. 168.

2. Susan Hardy Aiken, personal communication.

3. Sherry B. Ortner, "Is Female to Male as Nature Is to Culture?," in *Woman, Culture and Society*, ed. Michelle Zimbalist Rosaldo and Louise Lamphere (Stanford: Stanford University Press, 1978), p. 75.

4. Jane Gallop, *The Daughter's Seduction: Feminism and Psychoanalysis* (Ithaca: Cornell University Press, 1982), p. 47.

5. Ibid., p. 48.

6. Elaine Marks and Isabelle de Courtivron, eds., *New French Feminisms: An Anthology* (Amherst: University of Massachusetts Press, 1980), pp. 36–37. For exploration of this perverse female desire and *jouissance*, especially its self-sufficiency, see Luce Irigaray, "When Our Lips Speak Together," tr. Carolyn Burke, *Signs* 6 (Autumn 1980): 60–67.

7. Julia Kristeva, "Women's Time," tr. Alice Jardine and Harry Blake, *Signs* 7 (Autumn 1981): 33, 34, 42–43.

8. Domna C. Stanton, "Language and Revolution: The Franco-American Dis-Connection," in *The Future of Difference*, ed. Hester Eisenstein and Alice Jardine (Boston: G. K. Hall, 1980), p. 74.

9. Julia Kristeva, "Motherhood According to Bellini," *Desire in Language: A Semiotic Approach to Literature and Art*, ed. Leon S. Roudiez, tr. Thomas Gora, Alice Jardine, and Leon S. Roudiez (New York: Columbia University Press, 1980), p. 237.

10. Walter J. Ong, *Fighting for Life: Contest, Sexuality, and Consciousness* (Ithaca: Cornell University Press, 1981), p. 29.

11. Ibid., p. 140.

12. For a good discussion of the economic implications of aesthetic evaluations, see Barbara Herrnstein Smith, *Contingencies of Value* (Cambridge: Harvard University Press, 1989).

13. Lacan, *Feminine Sexuality*, p. 82.

14. Shoshana Felman, *Jacques Lacan and the Adventure of Insight: Psychoanalysis in Contemporary Culture* (Cambridge: Harvard University Press, 1987), p. 15.

WRITING (INTO) LIFE

1. Virginia Woolf, *A Writer's Diary* (New York: Harcourt Brace Jovanovich, 1954), p. 85.

2. Ibid., p. 144.

3. Doris Lessing, *The Memoirs of a Survivor* (New York: Bantam, 1976), p. 47.

4. Ibid., p. 60.

5. Ibid., pp. 200–201.

6. Ibid., p. 94.

7. Ibid., p. 14.

8. Ibid., pp. 101–2.

9. Ibid., p. 217.

10. Ibid., p. 4.

11. Virginia Woolf, *The Diary of Virginia Woolf*, vol. 1, *1915–1919*, ed. Anne Olivier Bell (New York: Harcourt Brace Jovanovich, 1977), p. 259.

12. Virginia Woolf, *The Years* (New York: Harcourt Brace Jovanovich, 1965), p. 435.

13. Virginia Woolf, *Three Guineas* (New York: Harcourt Brace Jovanovich, 1966), pp. 69–70.

14. Ibid., pp. 107, 114, 142, 143.

15. Woolf, *A Writer's Diary*, pp. 230–31.
16. Ibid., p. 435.
17. Virginia Woolf, *Between the Acts* (New York: Harcourt Brace Jovanovich, 1977), p. 57–58.
18. Ibid., p. 193.
19. Ibid., pp. 210–12.
20. Ibid., p. 219.
21. Lessing, *The Memoirs of a Survivor*, p. 216.
22. Woolf, *A Writer's Diary*, p. 179.

ESSAYING THE FEMININE

1. Virginia Woolf, *Three Guineas* (New York: Harcourt Brace Jovanovich, 1966), pp. 58, 107.
2. Julia Kristeva, "Women's Time," tr. Alice Jardine and Harry Blake, *Signs* 7 (Autumn 1981): 34.
3. Ibid., p. 35.
4. Domna C. Stanton, "Language and Revolution: The Franco-American Dis-Connection," in *The Future of Difference*, ed. Hester Eisenstein and Alice Jardin (Boston: G. K. Hall, 1980), p. 75.
5. Margaret Homans, " 'Her Very Own Howl': The Ambiguities of Representation in Recent Women's Fiction," *Signs* 9 (Winter 1983): 186, 187.
6. Stanton, "Language and Revolution," p. 76.
7. According to Stanton, ibid., p. 75.
8. Ibid., pp. 73, 80.
9. Michel de Montaigne, "Of Repentence," *Selections from the Essays*, ed. and tr. Donald M. Frame (Arlington Heights, Il.: AHM Publishing Corp., 1973), p. 75. Cf. Kristeva's notion of the subject "in process/on trial" (the French *procès* means both) in "Women's Time."
10. John O'Neill, *Essaying Montaigne: A Study of the Renais-*

sance Institution of Writing and Reading (London: Routledge and Kegan Paul, 1982), pp. 9, 32, 69.

11. Montaigne, "Of the Education of Children," in *Selections*, p. 10.

12. Montaigne, "To the Reader," in *Selections*, p. 3.

13. Montaigne, "Of Repentence," p. 76.

14. Francis Bacon, "The Four Idols," from *Novum Organum*, in *A World of Ideas*, ed. Lee A. Jacobus (New York: St. Martin's Press, 1983), p. 337.

15. Virginia Woolf, "Montaigne," *The Common Reader* (New York: Harcourt Brace & World, 1953), p. 66.

16. Virginia Woolf, "Professions for Women," *Women and Writing*, ed. Michèle Barrett (New York: Harcourt Brace Jovanovich, 1979), pp. 61, 62.

17. Virginia Woolf, "The Modern Essay," *The Common Reader*, p. 222.

18. Woolf, "Montaigne," p. 59.

19. Montaigne, "Of Repentence," p. 75.

20. Bacon, "The Four Idols," p. 332.

21. Gary Zukav, *The Dancing Wu Li Masters* (New York: Bantam Books, 1980), p. 31.

22. Michael Sprinker, "Fictions of the Self: The End of Autobiography," in *Autobiography: Essays Theoretical and Critical*, ed. James Olney (Princeton: Princeton University Press, 1980), p. 322.

23. Montaigne, "Of the Inconsistency of Our Actions," p. 48.

24. Louis A. Renza, "The Veto of the Imagination: A Theory of Autobiography," in *Autobiography*, pp. 272–73.

25. Ibid., p. 279.

26. Georges Gusdorf, "The Conditions and Limits of Autobiography," in *Autobiography*, p. 41.

27. Renza, "The Veto of the Imagination," p. 279.

28. Woolf, "Montaigne," p. 67.

29. Phyllis Rose, *Parallel Lives: Five Victorian Marriages* (New York: Alfred A. Knopf, 1983), p. 6.

30. Homans, "'Her Very Own Howl,'" p. 198.

31. Elaine Showalter, "Feminist Criticism in the Wilderness," *Critical Inquiry* 8 (Winter 1981): 200.

32. Elaine Marks and Isabelle de Courtivron, eds., *New French Feminism: An Anthology* (Amherst: University of Massachusetts Press, 1980), p. 4.

33. Homans, "'Her Very Own Howl,'" p. 200.

34. Sandra M. Gilbert and Susan Gubar, *The Madwoman in the Attic: The Woman Writer and the Nineteenth-Century Literary Imagination* (New Haven: Yale University Press, 1979), p. 6.

35. Adrienne Rich, "When We Dead Awaken: Writing as Revision," *On Lies, Secrets, and Silence: Selected Prose 1966–1978* (New York: W. W. Norton, 1978), p. 39.

36. Numerous explanations of this Lacanian account are available. For a particularly lucid one, see Terry Eagleton, *Literary Theory* (Minneapolis: University of Minnesota Press, 1983), pp. 163-74.

37. Jacqueline Rose, "Introduction—II," *Feminine Sexuality: Jacques Lacan and the école freudienne*, ed. Juliet Mitchell and Jacqueline Rose, tr. Jacqueline Rose (New York: W. W. Norton, 1982), p. 51.

38. Abby Frucht, "The Objects of My Invention," *The New York Times Book Review*, 11 April 1993, p. 24.

39. Russ Rymer, *Genie: An Abused Child's Flight from Silence* (New York: HarperCollins, 1993), p. 27.

40. Virginia Woolf, *A Room of One's Own* (New York: Harcourt Brace Jovanovich, 1957), p. 78.

41. Hélène Cixous, "Castration or Decapitation?" tr. Annette Kuhn, *Signs* 7 (Autumn 1981): 53.

42. Woolf, *A Room of One's Own*, p. 96.

43. Ibid., pp. 91, 96, 108.

44. For a study of this formative factor, see Louise DeSalvo, *Virginia Woolf: The Impact of Childhood Sexual Abuse on Her Life and Work* (Boston: Beacon Press, 1989).

45. Mary Daly, "New Archaic Afterwords," to *The Church and the Second Sex* (Boston: Beacon Press, 1985), p. xxvii.

IN SEARCH OF "IN SEARCH OF OUR MOTHERS' GARDENS"

1. Nelly Furman, "Textual Feminism," in *Women and Language in Literature and Society*, ed. Sally McConnell-Ginet, Ruth Borker, and Nelly Furman (New York: Praeger, 1980), p. 49.

2. Barbara Smith, "Toward a Black Feminist Criticism," in *All the Women Are White, All the Blacks Are Men, But Some of Us Are Brave*, ed. Gloria T. Hull, Patricia Bell Scott, and Barbara Smith (Old Westbury, N.Y.: The Feminist Press, 1982), p. 157.

3. Alice Walker, "*One* Child of One's Own: A Meaningful Digression Within the Work(s)," *In Search of Our Mother's Gardens* (New York: Harcourt Brace Jovanovich, 1983), p. 372. (All quotations from this collection are taken from this edition.)

4. Nancy Hoffman, "White Woman, Black Woman: Inventing an Adequate Pedagogy," *Women's Studies Newsletter* 5, 1 & 2 (Spring 1977): 21.

5. Margaret Homans, " 'Her Very Own Howl,': The Ambiguities of Representation in Recent Women's Fiction," *Signs* 9 (Winter 1983): 198.

6. Alice Walker, "In Search of Our Mothers' Gardens," *In Search of Our Mothers' Gardens*, p. 238.

7. Alice Walker, "From an Interview," *In Search of Our Mothers' Gardens*, p. 259.

8. Alice Walker, "The Divided Life of Jean Toomer," *In Search of Our Mothers' Gardens*, p. 61.

9. Virginia Woolf, *A Room of One's Own* (New York: Harcourt Brace Jovanovich, 1957), p. 2.

10. Elaine Showalter, "Feminist Criticism in the Wilderness," *Critical Inquiry* 8 (Winter 1981): 200.

11. Walker, "*One* Child of One's Own," p. 373.

READING HOUSES, WRITING LIVES

1. My editor at the publishing house that commissioned my first memoir, *Remembering the Bone House*, cut a good bit of my original draft for the introduction, "Reading Houses, Writing Lives," on the grounds that the quoted material, with its attendant footnotes, would alienate my readers. Although her editorial judgment, identical to that of the editor of *Plaintext*, was probably correct—given that her task was to develop marketable books and that the people drawn to personal narratives, especially ones involving chronic illness, may well not put up with feminist reflections, replete with footnotes, about literary themes—I felt torn as "life" was thus severed from "literature."

In part, I was disgusted at the way major trade publishers nowadays, assuming that readers are boobies, tend to search out risk-free material that the boobies will go for. I'm a reader myself, and I'm no booby. I hold my readers in no lower esteem than I hold myself. I read material with footnotes all the time (though I have to admit that since finishing my doctorate I'm not awfully systematic in footnote-reading), and so do most of the people I know. By imagining a marginally literate audience and insisting that writers address that audience in the hope of producing bestsellers, preferably ones that can be transformed into made-for-television movies, publishers bring out huge quantities of safe stuff. Not necessarily *bad* stuff, mind you—just generic—and after the forty-leventh tale about the husband's death, or the baby's death, or the mother's death, about the descent into madness, or alcohol, or paralysis, a dutiful reviewer may positively yearn for a "bad" book—something queer, off-kilter, surprising—even if it will never sell more than a couple of thousand copies.

But everyone who loves books has these reservations about publishing as "big business." The source of my distress went deeper, I think. I perceived in my editor's rejection of my more academic writing the message that the only part of me I could interest readers in (or enough readers anyway to interest the publisher's marketing people) was the damaged part. Now, physically there isn't very much left of me. To be whittled away intellectually as well strikes me straight through with grief and fear. And defiance. I am more than a slowly crumpling heap of flesh, and I think about more than its awful failure (though I think about that more than I would wish). In fact, I think most—now, as I have nearly all my life—about literature. I could not possibly write without the texts that give texture and context to my existence. So here all the footnotes are back.

2. Nancy Chodorow, *The Reproduction of Mothering: Psychoanalysis and the Sociology of Gender* (Berkeley and Los Angeles: University of California Press, 1978), p. 167.

3. Virginia Woolf, *A Writer's Diary* (New York: Harcourt Brace Jovanovich, 1954), p. 125.

4. Gaston Bachelard, *The Poetics of Space*, tr. Marie Joles (Boston: Beacon Press, 1969), p. xxxiii.

5. Ibid., pp. 5–6, 4.

6. Ibid., p. xix.

7. Hélène Cixous, "Sorties: Out and Out: Attacks/Ways Out/Forays," in *The Newly Born Woman*, tr. Betsy Wing (Minneapolis: University of Minnesota Press, 1986), p. 65.

8. Ibid., p. 65.

9. Cixous, "Sorties," p. 94.

10. Virginia Woolf, "Professions for Women," in *Women and Writing*, ed. Michele Barrett (New York: Harcourt Brace Jovanovich, 1979), pp. 61, 62.

11. Cixous, "Sorties," pp. 94, 97.

12. Bachelard, *The Poetics of Space*, p. 5.

13. Cixous, "Sorties," p. 68.

14. Ibid., p. 85.

15. Bachelard, *The Poetics of Space*, pp. 14–15.

16. For a discussion of temporal styles, see Julia Kristeva, "Women's Time," tr. Alice Jardine and Harry Blake, in *The Kristeva Reader*, ed. Toril Moi (New York: Columbia University Press, 1986), pp. 187–213.

17. Maurice Merleau-Ponty, *Signs*, tr. Richard C. McCleary (Evanston, Ill.: Northwestern University Press, 1964), p. 15.

18. Bachelard, *The Poetics of Space*, pp. 8, 9.

19. Cixous, "Sorties," pp. 85–86.

20. Merleau-Ponty, *Signs*, p. 175.

21. Ibid., p. 75.

22. Ibid., p. 59.

23. Sidonie Smith, *A Poetics of Women's Autobiography: Marginality and the Fictions of Self-Representation* (Bloomington and Indianapolis: Indiana University Press, 1987), p. 5.

24. Catherine Clément, "The Guilty One," in *The Newly Born Woman*, p. 55.

25. Merleau-Ponty, *Signs*, p. 112.

26. Bachelard, *The Poetics of Space*, p. 14.

THE LITERATURE OF PERSONAL DISASTER

1. Charles J. Sykes, *A Nation of Victims: The Decay of the American Character* (New York: St. Martin's Press, 1992), p. 15.

2. Cheri Register, *Living with Chronic Illness: Days of Patience and Passion* (New York: The Free Press, 1988).

3. Kate Millett, *The Loony-Bin Trip* (New York: Simon and Schuster, 1990), p. 285.

4. Sylvia Plath, "Blue Moles," *The Colossus* (New York: Vintage Books, 1968), p. 49.

5. Andre Dubus, *Broken Vessels* (Boston: David R. Godine, 1991), p. 138.

6. May Sarton, *After the Stroke* (New York: W. W. Norton, 1988), pp. 75–76, 42.

7. May Sarton, *Endgame* (New York: W. W. Norton, 1992), pp. 277–78.

8. Ibid., pp. 282, 186, 157.

THE WRITER'S THIN SKIN AND FAINT HEART

1. Virginia Woolf, *A Writer's Diary* (New York: Harcourt Brace Jovanovich, 1954), p. 11.

2. Ibid., p. 14.

3. Ibid., p. 59.

4. Virginia Woolf, *Three Guineas* (New York, Harcourt Brace Jovanovich, 1966), p. 80.

5. Woolf, *A Writer's Diary*, p. 206.

6. Ibid., p. 283.

7. Ibid., p. 15.

8. Susan Sherman, ed., *May Sarton: Among the Usual Days* (New York: W. W. Norton, 1993), p. 45.

9. Woolf, *A Writer's Diary*, p. 276.

10. Mary Oliver, "Spring," *New and Selected Poems* (Boston: Beacon Press, 1992), p. 70.

11. Woolf, *A Writer's Diary*, p. 46.

12. Ibid., p. 118.

13. Ibid., p. 131.

14. Sherman, *May Sarton*, p. 140.

Works

Cited

Bachelard, Gaston. *The Poetics of Space.* Translated by Marie Joles. Boston: Beacon Press, 1969.

Bacon, Francis. "The Four Idols," from *Novum Organum.* In *A World of Ideas*, edited by Lee A. Jacobus. New York: St. Martin's Press, 1983.

Chodorow, Nancy. *The Reproduction of Mothering: Psychoanalysis and the Sociology of Gender.* Berkeley and Los Angeles: University of California Press, 1978.

Cixous, Hélène. "Castration or Decapitation?" Translated by Annette Kuhn. *Signs* 7 (Autumn 1981).

Cixous, Hélène. "Sorties: Out and Out: Attacks/Ways Out/Forays." In *The Newly Born Woman*, translated by Betsy Wing. Minneapolis: University of Minnesota Press, 1986.

Clément, Catherine. "The Guilty One." In *The Newly Born*

Woman, translated by Betsy Wing. Minneapolis: University of Minnesota Press, 1986.

Daly, Mary. *The Church and the Second Sex*. Boston: Beacon Press, 1985.

DeSalvo, Louise. *Virginia Woolf: The Impact of Childhood Sexual Abuse on Her Life and Work*. Boston: Beacon Press, 1989.

Dubus, Andre. *Broken Vessels* Boston: David R. Godine, 1991.

Eagleton, Terry. *Literary Theory*. Minneapolis: University of Minnesota Press, 1983.

Felman, Shoshana. *Jacques Lacan and the Adventure of Insight: Psychoanalysis in Contemporary Culture*. Cambridge, Mass.: Harvard University Press, 1987.

Frucht, Abby. "The Objects of My Invention." *The New York Times Book Review*, 11 April 1993.

Furman, Nelly. "Textual Feminism." In *Women and Language in Literature and Society*, edited by Sally McConnell-Ginet, Ruth Borker, and Nelly Furman. New York: Praeger, 1980.

Gallop, Jane. *The Daughter's Seduction: Feminism and Psychoanalysis*. Ithaca: Cornell University Press, 1982.

Gilbert, Sandra M., and Susan Gubar. *The Madwoman in the Attic: The Woman Writer and the Nineteenth-Century Literary Imagination*. New Haven, Con.: Yale University Press, 1979.

Gusdorf, Georges. "The Conditions and Limits of Autobiography." In *Autobiography: Essays Theoretical and Critical*, edited by James Olney. Princeton: Princeton University Press, 1980.

Heilbrun, Carolyn. *Writing a Woman's Life*. New York: W. W. Norton, 1988.

Hoffman, Nancy. "White Woman, Black Woman: Inventing an Adequate Pedagogy." *Women's Studies Newsletter* 5, 1 & 2 (Spring 1977).

Homans, Margaret, " 'Her Very Own Howl': The Ambiguities of Representation in Recent Women's Fiction.' *Signs* 9 (Winter 1983).

Irigaray, Luce. "When Our Lips Speak Together." Translated by Carolyn Burke. *Signs* 6 (Autumn 1980).

163

Jardine, Alice A. *Gynesis: Configurations of Woman and Modernity*. Ithaca: Cornell University Press, 1985.

Kristeva, Julia. *Desire in Language: A Semiotic Approach to Literature and Art.* Edited by Leon S. Roudiez; translated by Thomas Gora, Alice Jardine, and Leon S. Roudiez. New York: Columbia University Press, 1980.

———. *The Kristeva Reader*. Edited by Toril Moi. New York: Columbia University Press, 1986.

Lacan, Jacques. *Feminine Sexuality*. Edited by Juliet Mitchell and Jacqueline Rose; translated by Jacqueline Rose. New York: W. W. Norton, 1982.

Lessing, Doris. *The Memoirs of a Survivor*. New York: Bantam, 1976.

Marks, Elaine, and Isabelle de Courtivron, eds. *New French Feminisms: An Anthology*. Amherst: University of Massachusetts Press, 1980.

Merleau-Ponty, Maurice. *Signs*. Translated by Richard C. McCleary. Evanston, Ill.: Northwestern University Press, 1964.

Millett, Kate. *The Loony-Bin Trip*. New York: Simon and Schuster, 1990.

Moi, Toril. *Sexual/Textual Politics: Feminist Literary Theory*. London and New York: Routledge, 1988.

Montaigne, Michel de. *Selections from the Essays*. Edited and translated by Donald M. Frame. Arlington Heights, Ill.: AHM Publishing Corp., 1973.

Oliver Mary. *New and Selected Poems*. Boston: Beacon Press, 1992.

O'Neill, John. *Essaying Montaigne: A Study of the Renaissance Institution of Writing and Reading*. London: Routledge and Kegan Paul, 1982.

Ong, Walter J. *Fighting for Life: Contest, Sexuality, and Consciousness*. Ithaca: Cornell University Press, 1981.

Ortner, Sherry B. "Is Female to Male as Nature Is to Culture?" In *Woman, Culture, and Society*, edited by Michelle Zimbalist Rosaldo and Louise Lamphere. Stanford: Stanford University Press, 1978.

Plath, Sylvia. *The Colossus*. New York: Vintage Books, 1968.

Register, Cheri. *Living with Chronic Illness: Days of Patience and Passion*. New York: The Free Press, 1988.

Renza, Louis A. "The Veto of the Imagination: A Theory of Autobiography." In *Autobiography: Essays Theoretical and Critical*, edited by James Olney. Princeton: Princeton University Press, 1980.

Rich, Adrienne. *On Lies, Secrets, and Silence: Selected Prose 1966–1978*. New York: W. W. Norton, 1978.

Rose, Phyllis. *Parallel Lives: Five Victorian Marriages*. New York: Alfred A. Knopf, 1983.

Ruether, Rosemary Radford. *Disputed Questions: On Being a Christian*. New York: Orbis Books, 1989.

Rymer, Russ. *Genie: An Abused Child's Flight from Silence*. New York: HarperCollins, 1993.

Sarton, May. *After the Stroke*. New York: W. W. Norton, 1988.

————. *Endgame*. New York: W. W. Norton, 1992.

Sherman, Susan, ed. *May Sarton: Among the Usual Days*. New York, W. W. Norton, 1993.

Showalter, Elaine. "Feminist Criticism in the Wilderness." *Critical Inquiry* 8 (Winter 1981).

Smith, Barbara. "Toward a Black Feminist Criticism." In *All the Women Are White, All the Blacks Are Men, But Some of Us Are Brave*, edited by Gloria T. Hull, Patricia Bell Scott, and Barbara Smith. Old Westbury, N.Y.: The Feminist Press, 1982.

Smith, Barbara Herrnstein. *Contingencies of Value*. Cambridge, Mass.: Harvard University Press, 1989.

Smith, Sidonie. *A Poetics of Women's Autobiography: Marginality and the Fictions of Self-Representation*. Bloomington and Indianapolis: Indiana University Press, 1987.

Sprinker, Michael. "Fictions of the Self: The End of Autobiography." In *Autobiography: Essays Theoretical and Critical*, edited by James Olney. Princeton: Princeton University Press, 1980.

Stanton, Domna C. "Language and Revolution: The Franco-

American Dis-Connection." In *The Future of Difference*, edited by Hester Eisenstein and Alice Jardine. Boston: G. K. Hall, 1980.

Sykes, Charles J. *A Nation of Victims: The Decay of the American Character*. New York: St. Martin's Press, 1992.

Tompkins, Jane. "Me and My Shadow." In *Gender and Theory: Dialogues on Feminist Criticism*, edited by Linda Kaufman. New York: Basil Blackwell, 1989.

Walker, Alice. *In Search of Our Mother's Gardens*. New York: Harcourt Brace Jovanovich, 1983.

Woolf, Virginia. *Between the Acts*. New York: Harcourt Brace Jovanovich, 1977.

———. *The Common Reader*. New York: Harcourt, Brace & World, 1953.

———. *The Diary of Virginia Woolf*. Vol. 1, *1915–1919*. Edited by Anne Olivier Bell. New York: Harcourt Brace Jovanovich, 1977.

———. *A Room of One's Own* (New York: Harcourt Brace Jovanovich, 1957.

———. *Three Guineas*. New York: Harcourt Brace Jovanovich, 1966.

———. *Women and Writing*. Edited by Michele Barrett. New York: Harcourt Brace Jovanovich, 1979.

———. *A Writer's Diary*. New York: Harcourt Brace Jovanovich, 1954.

———. *The Years*. New York: Harcourt Brace Jovanovich, 1965.

Zukav, Gary. *The Dancing Wu Li Masters*. New York: Bantam Books, 1980.